T0080482

Powerful Phrases for Dealing with Difficult People

Powerful Phrases for Dealing with Difficult People

Over 325 Ready-to-Use Words and Phrases for Working with Challenging Personalities

Renée Evenson

HarperCollins
Leadership

An Imprint of HarperCollins

Powerful Phrases for Dealing with Difficult People

© 2014 Renée Evenson

All rights reserved. No portion of this book may be reproduced, stored in a retrieval system, or transmitted in any form or by any means—electronic, mechanical, photocopy, recording, scanning, or other—except for brief quotations in critical reviews or articles, without the prior written permission of the publisher.

Published by HarperCollins Leadership, an imprint of HarperCollins Focus LLC.

Any internet addresses, phone numbers, or company or product information printed in this book are offered as a resource and are not intended in any way to be or to imply an endorsement by HarperCollins Leadership, nor does HarperCollins Leadership vouch for the existence, content, or services of these sites, phone numbers, companies, or products beyond the life of this book.

ISBN 978-0-8144-3298-3 (TP)

Printed in the United States of America

CONTENTS

PART 1
Powerful Phrases + Actions = Successful
Work Relationships

PART 2
Effective Conflict Resolution = Strengthened Work Relationships

5 Powerful Phrases for Challenging Situations with Your Boss 155

6 Powerful Phrases for Situations You Cause 207

About the Author 225

ACKNOWLEDGMENTS

I'd like to thank all the employees at AMACOM Books who took part in producing this book. You're a great team—*not* at all difficult to deal with —and I've enjoyed working with each of you on this project.

In particular, I'd like to offer a heartfelt thanks to my editor at AMACOM Books, Bob Nirkind, who has been supportive and encouraging as we worked together to create this book. I couldn't have asked for a better editor on this project, as I always enjoy working with you.

From the bottom of my heart, thank you to my production editor, Barbara Chernow. I appreciate the care and attention you give to each of my books. I know they're in the best of hands with you.

My gratitude goes to my husband Joe and to my family and friends. Thanks to each of you for your input on this project.

And my appreciation is sent to the readers of my books. My aim always is to help others improve their talents and abilities. If I help you deal better with difficult people, then I've achieved my goal.

Powerful Phrases for
Dealing with Difficult People

Introduction

The ability to conduct yourself harmoniously and productively with your employees, colleagues, and bosses is a critical skill to master. However, when you enter the working world, no one equips you with this skillset, particularly as it applies to dealing with people who are difficult. When different personality types are expected to work side by side every day and get along with each other, it can be challenging. You can choose your friends, but you can't choose those with whom you work and, when you spend most of your waking hours with people who aren't of your choosing, getting along may prove to be demanding.

Yet, your ability to maintain strong work relationships is so important; it may, in fact, be vital to your success. Often, an employee who is capable of interacting well with others will be promoted over an employee who possesses greater job or technical knowledge. The ability to relate successfully to others doesn't necessarily mean being agreeable all the time, because we know that problems are going to arise. Rather, it's having the skills to effectively deal with those problems that will set you apart as an employee who values the importance of resolving conflict to maintain strong relationships.

Conflict is one of the most difficult situations we face because it thrusts us out of our comfort zone. The truth is that most of us are uncomfortable handling conflict of any kind, so we overlook problems and hope they'll go away. But that never happens. Unless you work to resolve conflict in an effective manner, one of two things is going to occur: Your working relationship with that person will be permanently damaged, or you'll bottle up your emotions and continue trying to ignore the problem. A damaged working relationship will never rectify itself; instead, the relationship will continue to fracture and may eventually sever completely. Further, when you bottle up your emotions, they slowly simmer until one day they begin to boil, which may cause you to lose control in an eruption of words you'll later regret.

A more effective way exists to handle conflict at work. Entering into a constructive conversation to resolve any problem as it occurs is the only way to demonstrate your ability to interact well with others all the time . . . and increase your odds for success.

In *Powerful Phrases for Dealing with Difficult People,* you'll find the tools that will enable you to develop the skills to handle any type of conflict with any person. You'll learn how to gain the cooperation of co-workers who are know-it-alls, meeting monopolizers, and people who send excessive emails. You'll learn how to communicate effectively with a boss who may be abusive, egotistical, micromanaging, or noncommunicative. And, when you cause a problem, you'll learn how to quickly recover, regroup, and work to successfully resolve the issue and reconcile the relationship.

In this book, you'll learn how to use over 325 powerful phrases to communicate effectively, as well as powerful actions to take in support of those phrases. You'll become familiar with the five-step process to resolve conflict of any kind. In addition, you'll develop the ability to work through problems with 30 types of difficult behaviors and personalities. And, throughout the book, you'll find "Something to Think About" tips, which detail how to handle unusual or difficult situations. The powerful words and phrases will be noted in *italics* and the type of phrase or word in **bold.**

Part 1, "Powerful Phrases + Actions = Successful Work Relationships," explains the phrases and nonverbal techniques that form the basis of communicating effectively to resolve conflict. You'll learn when to incorporate "I" phrases to communicate how the problem affected you, along with words and phrases of understanding, apology, compromise, resolution, and reconciliation. You'll ascertain the body language, facial expressions, tone of voice, and assertiveness actions that will enhance your conversation.

Both chapters in Part 1 include *Resolving Conflict: The Wrong Way/ Why This Doesn't Work* and *Resolving Conflict: The Right Way/Why This Works* sample dialogues to reinforce how the phrases and actions you're learning will be advantageous when handling any type of disagreement you encounter. Both chapters also include a summary of sample phrases and nonverbal techniques, which will be beneficial for quick reference.

Part 2, "Effective Conflict Resolution = Strengthened Work Relationships," builds on the powerful words and phrases and nonverbal techniques in Part 1 to show you when and how to incorporate them into your conflict resolution conversations. In Chapter 3, you'll learn the five-step technique to resolve any conflict. Included in this chapter are *Resolving Conflict: The Wrong Way/ Why This Doesn't Work* and *Resolving Conflict: The Right Way/Why This Works* sample dialogues, as well as a summary of the key points for each of the steps.

Chapters 4 and 5 describe 20 challenging coworker behaviors and 10 challenging personality types of bosses. You'll discover how to use the five-step process to confront conflict and effectively resolve problems. Sample *Resolving Conflict: The Right Way/Why This Works* dialogues take you through each step of the process. These chapters also include "Applying the Approach," a quick reference of helpful tips for dealing with each of the behaviors and personality types.

In Chapter 6, you'll learn how to handle situations in which you caused a problem. When you realize you've said or done something inappropriate, offensive, or unkind, you'll be prepared to take the initiative and incorporate powerful phrases and words in conversations to repair and reconcile the relationship. And, when someone approaches you about a problem you didn't realize you caused, you'll learn how to quickly recover and work through the five-steps to resolve the conflict, no matter whether the person approaches you in a constructive manner or confronts you in a spiteful or hurtful manner.

Powerful Phrases for Dealing with Difficult People will be your guide when you encounter problems with your employees, colleagues, or bosses. You'll be able to specifically identify the behaviors and personality types that are problematic for you. You'll build your confidence to handle any type of conflict with any person, whether you have a problem with someone or another person has a problem with you. It's the book that will provide you with the skills to enter into a productive dialogue and resolve any problem quickly.

Powerful Phrases for Dealing with Difficult People will enhance your communication skills, improve your leadership skills, and increase your assertiveness skills. When you develop these skills, you'll be seen as a person who connects successfully with others. And that is going to strengthen all of your work relationships.

Powerful Phrases + Actions = Successful Work Relationships

PART

1

Powerful Phrases
+ Actions =
Successful Work
Relationships

Communicating
Powerful Phrases

Trying to get along with coworkers and bosses can be difficult at best. However, since you probably spend more of your waking hours at work than you do at home, it makes good business sense to get along with everyone. But when you're forced to interact all day with people who, let's face it, may not be people you'd choose to be with, they can test your mettle, tick you off, and sour your attitude.

The bottom line is that no matter how well you get along with people, you aren't going to get along with everyone all the time. Whenever people spend a lot of time together, conflicts are going to arise. But, in work situations, the conflicts can be particularly tough to handle. It's hard to maintain your composure and self-control when a coworker's done something that's irritated you, but that's just what you need to do.

Employees who are able to stay calm and approach conflict in a self-controlled, thoughtful manner are viewed more positively by coworkers and bosses. When you take the time to think before speaking, plan the best approach to handle the problem, and communicate in a constructive manner, your coworkers and bosses are more likely to listen and respond considerately to you.

If you're uncomfortable facing conflict, you're not alone. Most people feel uncomfortable when dealing with these situations and hope the problem will just go away. The bad news is that ignoring conflict will only aggravate the problem, often to the point where even a minor problem becomes unmanageable. It's like the straw that breaks the camel's back! If left unresolved, conflict can make you disgruntled and bitter; it can cause work relationships to breakdown completely; and it can spill over into and negatively affect your interactions with customers, vendors, and other business contacts. And, in the worst-case scenario, unresolved conflicts at work may even affect your personal relationships.

So what happens when the people you work with—and for—aren't easy to get along with? What do you do when your coworkers won't assume responsibility for their actions, like to gossip, take credit for your work, talk too loudly, or bully others? What do you do when your boss piles on the work, berates you in front of coworkers, plays favorites, or possesses zero percent job knowledge? And what happens when it isn't your coworkers or boss who cause the problem? What do you do when you're the cause of the situation? You may inadvertently say or do something and realize later that it may have been upsetting to the other person. Or, you may not even realize your blunder until the other person confronts you about it. Knowing how to quickly recover and resolve conflict when you're the cause enables you to keep your work relationships constructive and productive.

When you arm yourself with the skills to begin a positive dialogue when faced with conflict; to communicate assertively, confidently, and constructively to uncover the cause of the problem; and to work toward a solution that's agreeable to everyone, you'll gain the cooperation and respect of your coworkers and upper management. Further, you'll be seen as an employee who's committed to being part of the solution rather than part of the problem.

This chapter focuses on the basics of communicating when facing conflict: the powerful phrases you'll use when confronting and discussing a problem with a coworker or boss. These phrases even work when you have a disagreement with a friend or family member!

Knowing the right phrases to use to communicate may make all the difference between effectively resolving conflict and furthering an already difficult situation. Learning how to incorporate powerful phrases into your vocabulary is the first step to help you resolve disharmony at work.

Resolving Conflict: The Wrong Way

During a staff meeting, Kate was in the middle of her presentation when Emma, one of her coworkers, interrupted and disagreed with what she was saying. As a result, Kate lost her concentration and confidence and found it difficult to regroup and get back on track. Kate became upset and angry, especially since Emma had interrupted her in a previous meeting.

Kate's been stewing about it since the meeting. Therefore, when she saw Emma in the hallway, she blurted out: "You know, you always interrupt me during my presentations. Yesterday you did it again! You jumped in before I finished and started disagreeing with me. It really bugs me every time you do that."

"I don't *always* interrupt you," Emma snapped. "And, maybe if you said something that made sense, I wouldn't need to disagree with you."

"Well, next time keep your thoughts to yourself until I'm done talking, okay?" Kate responded.

"Who do you think you are?" Emma countered. "I have a right to my opinion and if you're talking nonsense, I'm going to speak up." Emma turned and huffed off, leaving Kate fuming.

Why This Doesn't Work

This conversation wasn't going to end well from the moment Kate accused Emma of always interrupting her. Emma immediately went on the defensive, the conversation heated up, and the interaction went quickly downhill. Both women spoke angrily, and there was no way to transform their banter into a constructive dialogue. When Emma stomped away and left Kate incensed, the problem wasn't resolved and, more importantly, their relationship suffered. Kate did get her point across about how the interruptions bugged her, and Emma may be mindful not to interrupt her in the future, but it's likely that these co-workers will have a difficult time getting along and working together.

Something to Think About

When confronting someone, refrain from using the words *always* or *never*. When you say to someone: "You always…" or "You never…," the other person is going to focus more on that one word than on the point you're trying to make and is likely to become instantly defensive, as Emma did. Rarely is anything *always* or *never*.

Begin with "I" Phrases

The number one rule when resolving conflict is never to open a conversation with the word *you*. Doing so may result in anger, yelling, hurling accusations back and forth, or someone stomping off. The *you* word is going to immediately put the other person on the defensive. Think about it. Has anyone said something like this to you: "You talk too much! No one else can get a word in" or "You never take responsibility for your mistakes." Your likely response is to defend yourself and fight back. "No, I don't! Bob talks just as much, if not more, than I do." or "Yes I do. And what about you? I'm always fixing your errors." This is definitely not the way to begin a conversation when you're trying to resolve a problem.

When you're having an issue with another person and decide to discuss it with him or her, it's difficult to have a productive conversation when you lead off with an accusatory statement or one that sounds as though you're blaming the person for the problem. When you confront someone who's done something that bugs you, keep the focus on "I" rather than on "you." Think about how the person's behavior made you feel. Open the conversation with an "I" statement describing how the event affected you, and you'll come across in a more constructive manner. After all: "I'm" the one with the problem. "You" may not even know that what you're doing that bugs me.

Sample "I" Phrases

You don't want your opening statement to sound like an attack the other person's character, so always begin with an "I" phrase:

- *"I was hurt when you said I make too many mistakes."*
- *"I became upset when you took credit for my work."*
- *"I felt betrayed when I heard that you talked behind my back."*
- *"I became confused and lost focus when you interrupted me during my sales presentation."*
- *"I was surprised when you jumped in before I had time to finish."*
- *"I get frustrated every time you talk so loudly that I can't hear my customers."*

> ## Something to Think About
>
> If you don't know how to launch into your conversation, try prefacing your "I" phrase by saying something like: *"I have something I need to talk to you about"* or *"I have something I need to get off my chest"* or *"Something happened that's been bothering me."*

Incorporating "I" Phrases

Here's a sample of how Kate could have opened the conversation using an "I" phrase:

"I have something I want to talk to you about. Yesterday during our meeting, I became upset when I was in the middle of my presentation and you disagreed with what I was saying. That really threw me off track for the rest of my presentation."

Had Kate begun her conversation with Emma in this manner, the dialogue would have headed in a different direction. Kate stated what happened and painted the picture of how it affected her presentation. Emma is likely to focus on Kate's feelings and doing so will lessen the need to defend herself. After listening to Kate, Emma would have either understood where her coworker was coming from ... or not. Either way, Kate would have taken a positive first step to discussing and effectively resolving the conflict.

Emma may have responded: "Gee, I'm sorry. I didn't mean to do that."

Or, she may have said: "I didn't agree with what you were saying and felt it was important to voice my opinion before you went further."

The first scenario will likely resolve itself when adding phrases of understanding and resolution (as you'll learn in the following sections). Emma appreciated how Kate felt, took responsibility, apologized, and will be more conscious not to interrupt her in the future.

In the second scenario, Emma heard how Kate felt but failed to take responsibility for her actions. In this case, Kate will need to continue her discussion to effectively resolve the conflict; otherwise, Emma is likely to do it again and Kate is likely to become upset again.

Phrases of Understanding

Opening your conversation with "I" phrases keeps the focus on how the other person's actions made you feel. After listening to that person's response, it's important to let the person know you understand that he or she may view the situation differently. By doing this, you demonstrate that you're willing to listen to the other perspective before drawing your conclusion or assigning blame.

When you show others you understand they may have a different viewpoint, you open the door to having a productive conversation. Conveying understanding is also a great way to build a rapport. You and the other person may be able to find common ground, and it may also encourage the other person to look at the problem from your vantage point. After listening to you, he or she may respond, "You know, now that I'm thinking about it, I wouldn't like that done to me either."

In addition, offering a phrase of understanding allows you to step into the other person's shoes for a moment. Let's say that a coworker has been short tempered with you. It's been bugging you because you can't think of anything you did to cause the person to treat you this way, so you offered an "I" phrase and your coworker said he was sorry. Then you offered a phrase of understanding such as: "I realize you didn't do that on purpose, but it made me wonder if I said or did something that bothered you." Saying this encourages your coworker to give you more information: "No, it's not you. My mother had a pretty serious operation and since she was released from the hospital I've been staying with her. I'm beyond exhausted and running on empty." You have an *aha* moment. In this scenario, offering a phrase of understanding and walking in your coworker's shoes put everything in perspective.

Sample Phrases of Understanding

You can follow up an "I" phrase with a phrase of understanding in situations in which the other person didn't take responsibility for his or her actions or doesn't seem to understand your feelings.

- *"I realize that you didn't do it on purpose."*
- *"I understand that you didn't mean it to sound that way."*
- *"I'm sure you were just excited when you started talking."*
- *"I'm certain you didn't mean to take credit for my idea."*
- *"I know you well enough to know that you wouldn't knowingly do that to me."*

You can also use a phrase of understanding when you have an *aha* moment. Incorporating a phrase of understanding at that point will productively move the conversation along.

- *"Now I see where you're coming from."*
- *"I understand the situation from your viewpoint now."*
- *"I can see why you didn't think that would bother me."*
- *"I'm glad you gave me the additional information. I realize why you did that."*

Incorporating Phrases of Understanding

After Emma apologized in the first scenario, Kate offered a phrase of understanding: *"I figured you didn't know that would be upsetting to me."* Both women have a better appreciation of the situation, and it's not likely to happen again.

But in the second scenario, when Emma didn't take responsibility, Kate said: *"Look, I realize that you wouldn't do that on purpose to upset me."* The ball is in Emma's court now. She responded: "Of course I didn't do it to upset you. I didn't know if I'd have the opportunity to voice my opinion if I didn't speak up right away." They now have a constructive dialogue going.

Phrases of Apology

Saying I'm sorry doesn't necessarily mean saying you're wrong. Saying I'm sorry means you're the one who's taking responsibility for resolving the conflict and mending the relationship. You might offer an apology to explain your state of mind, how you feel about what happened, or why you felt the need to bring up the issue.

Offering a phrase of apology can go a long way in opening the lines of communication and productively moving the dialogue along. A sincere apology holds a great deal of power. It can diffuse anger, lessen pride, and soothe hurt feelings. You won't always need to incorporate a phrase of apology into your conflict resolution conversation, but if you feel it'll help move the dialogue along, why not? Whenever you're at a stalemate in your discussion and the other person isn't willing to budge or look at the situation from your perspective, offering an apology can often change a person's disposition.

Sample Phrases of Apology

Offer a phrase of apology whenever you feel it will encourage empathy between the other person and you.

- *"I'm sorry if I seem overly sensitive."*
- *"I'm sorry if I misunderstood your intent."*

- *"I'm sorry that we need to have this conversation."*
- *"I apologize if I misunderstood what happened."*
- *"I regret that I have to bring this up."*
- *"Please forgive me for feeling this way."*

Incorporating Phrases of Apology

In the first scenario, Emma apologized and took responsibility. As a result, the conflict was resolved, so there was no need for Kate to return the apology. In the second scenario, Emma didn't take responsibility. So, after offering a phrase of understanding, Kate added: *"I'm sorry if this seems trivial."* In saying this, Kate let Emma know that she not only understood that they viewed the situation differently, but that she wanted Emma to respond so that she'd have a better idea of where Emma stood on the issue.

Phrases of Compromise

Compromise is the optimum way to resolve conflict. People are usually able to reach a compromise when they remain flexible, ask questions to gain a better understanding of the situation, listen with an open mind, look at the circumstance from the other person's perspective, and try to find middle ground. When people who are in a conflict discussion are able to compromise, the chances of agreeing on a solution greatly increase.

Communicating phrases of compromise means that you want to negotiate fairly and find the best solution and that you're willing to remain open as you work toward an agreement. Phrases of compromise demonstrate that you want to cooperate, listen, and find middle ground. When you're willing to cooperate, others will be more apt to cooperate with you. When you're open to listening, others will be more apt to listen to you. And when you're trying to find middle ground, others will be more apt to meet you halfway. When those things occur, you're on your way to negotiating a suitable conclusion.

Sample Phrases of Compromise

When you open your conversation with an "I" phrase and offer a phrase of understanding and your colleague doesn't take responsibility, you'll want to add a phrase of compromise to continue the dialogue.

- *"Let's talk about this. I need to know why it happened and how we can keep it from happening again."*
- *"Can we talk about what happened?"*
- *"I feel that we need to talk this out so it doesn't happen again."*
- *"Let's go somewhere in private and try to resolve this."*
- *"Let's talk this over and find a suitable compromise."*
- *"I'd like to hear how you saw the situation so that I better understand."*

During your discussion to resolve the problem, it's important to remain flexible so you'll want to incorporate additional phrases of compromise.

- *"Here's how you see the issue: _____. And here's how I see it: _____. Let's see where we can come together on this."*
- *"Since we don't agree why this happened, let's lay out the facts and come up with a solution we both can live with."*
- *"Why don't we each state our viewpoints? Then we'll see if we can find common ground."*
- *"We need to resolve this somehow. The only way to do that is for each of us to be flexible and try to come together."*

Incorporating Phrases of Compromise

In the first scenario, Emma took responsibility, the problem resolved itself, and further discussion wasn't necessary. In the second scenario, however, Kate needed to further the conversation. So she chose phrases of apology, stating that she knew Emma might find the matter trivial. And, Emma replied: "Yeah, I do think it's trivial."

Kate had prepared herself for this type of response and said: "To me it wasn't trivial. Do you have a few minutes now? *I'd like to talk this over and find an agreeable solution.* (**compromise**) Let's go into the conference room where we can talk in private."

After closing the door, Kate said: *"Why don't we try to look at the situation from each other's viewpoint? That may help us find an agreeable solution."* (**compromise**)

"Okay, sure. You don't like me disagreeing with you, and I felt it was important to voice my opinion."

"That's not what bothered me. *I understand that we're not always going to agree.* (**understanding**) What bothered me was that you interrupted me during the middle of my presentation, and it really threw me off track. I would have appreciated if you waited until I was done speaking to voice your disagreement."

"I'm sorry if I threw you off track. That would have bothered me too. It's just that I didn't know if I'd have the chance if I waited. In another meeting I did wait and when you finished speaking, the discussion changed direction and I wasn't able to make my point."

"Oh, I can understand how frustrating that must have been. (**understanding**) *How does this sound? From now on, if you'll allow me to finish my presentation without interrupting, I'll see to it that we don't move on to another topic before asking if anyone would like to add something. That way, you'll be able to voice your opinion."* (**compromise**)

"That works for me."

Something to Think About

Timing is important when you're trying to resolve conflict of any kind, so before beginning your discussion, make sure it's a good time. When Kate asked Emma if she had a few minutes to talk, she made sure that Emma was open to having the conversation at that time. If now isn't a good time for the other person, ask when it will be and then schedule a time that's agreeable to both of you.

Phrases of Resolution

As you saw in the previous scenario, the coworkers were able to calmly discuss the situation, talk through the problem, and reach a compromise. That's how many conflict resolution discussions go. When each of the involved parties is able to voice their opinion, listen to each other's perspective, compromise, and agree on a solution, everyone feels good about the outcome.

Offering a phrase of resolution is an important next step. You want to make sure that everyone truly is in agreement about the outcome and, in the event that you aren't able to garner agreement from all the involved parties, you want to make sure that everyone understands why this is the best solution.

For example, during a discussion on the best way to resolve billing mistakes, you agree to manage it at the point of contact, but one member of your team feels that the employee who was responsible for the error should handle the problem. As the meeting winds down, you need to gain the hold-out's agreement to the resolution by explaining why that solution was chosen: *"Look, Josh, we understand that you feel differently.* **(understanding)** But, if we turn the contact over to another employee, there's going to be a delay in getting the problem resolved. It'll take extra time to explain the situation. And, what if the employee's on vacation? *Since the rest of us feel this is the best way to handle these errors, can you live with our decision?*" (**resolution**) Josh responds: "I see your point. In the past we've been inconsistent in handling these types of problems but as long as we're all handling them the same way, then I'll agree."

Sample Phrases of Resolution

After finding a solution that's agreeable to all parties, add a phrase of resolution to show your appreciation that you were able to reach an agreement.

- *"I'm happy . . . we could resolve this."*
- *"I'm glad . . . we talked this out. We have a better understanding of what happened."*
- *"I'm pleased . . . we were able to clear up the misunderstanding."*
- *"I'm thrilled . . . we were able to come to an agreement."*

If you're not sure the solution is agreeable to everyone, voice your phrase of resolution as a question.

- *"Are you satisfied with the solution?"*
- *"Is there anything else we need to talk about?"*
- *"Do you feel we have a better understanding of what caused the problem?"*
- *"How do you feel about the solution?"*
- *"I'm happy with our compromise. How do you feel about it?"*

Incorporating Phrases of Resolution

In the first scenario in which Emma took responsibility, Kate added a phrase of resolution: *"I'm glad we talked this out."*

And in second scenario, when Emma responded: "That works for me," she was stating that an agreement had been reached. Kate felt good that they reached a compromise, and she said: *"I'm glad we talked this out."* Then she restated the resolution: *"Now I have a better understanding of your viewpoint. After finishing any future presentations, I'll make sure you get a chance to speak up, even if it is to disagree with me!"* (**resolution**) They laughed, and both felt good that they were able to resolve the problem.

Something to Think About

It's a good idea to restate the resolution just in case you misinterpreted what you and your coworker agreed to.

Phrases of Reconciliation

Whenever you talk through a problem, show understanding, compromise, and reach a resolution, you should feel proud that you effectively and successfully resolved the problem. You began your conversation with an "I" phrase and a phrase of understanding. You may or may not have felt the need to apologize. You then incorporated phrases of compromise during your discussion and, after reaching agreement, followed up with a phrase of resolution.

Before ending the discussion, take one more step and say something about the value of your working relationship. Letting the other person know that he or she is important to you ends your conversation on a positive note and will strengthen your working relationship.

Sample Phrases of Reconciliation

Always end your conflict resolution discussions with a positive comment about your relationship.

- *"I value our working relationship. . . . Going forward I feel we'll be able to work through any problem."*
- *"I'm glad we talked this out. . . . Now I'm confident we can work through any problem."*
- *"I respect you . . . and know that we'll work even more closely now."*
- *"I'm glad we talked this out.... In the future, we're not going to let any disagreement get in the way of our friendship."*
- *"I have a better understanding of you . . ., and I hope you do of me as well."*
- *"We've always worked closely and going forward.... I know that we won't let a little problem stand between us."*

Incorporating Phrases of Reconciliation

After offering a phrase of resolution, Kate said: *"I'm so glad we talked this out. I value our working relationship and wouldn't want anything to detract from that."* **(reconciliation)** They both left the meeting pleased with the outcome and feeling comfortable that they'll be able to work through any problem.

Resolving Conflict: The Right Way

After Emma interrupted Kate once again and disagreed with what she was saying, Kate became upset. She found it difficult to regroup but managed to complete her presentation without outwardly appearing shaken or upset. Since this had happened before, Kate saw a pattern emerging. On the surface, it appeared to her that Emma didn't respect her. Kate felt it was time to confront the situation, but before speaking she first considered how to best approach Emma. She also thought through possible conversations that might ensue.

The next day, Kate and Emma were talking. Kate waited for a lull in the conversation, and then said: *"I have something I want to talk to you about. Yesterday during our meeting, I became upset when I was in the middle of my presentation and you disagreed with what I was saying. That really threw me off track for the rest of my presentation."* (**"I" phrase**)

Kate hoped that Emma would understand where she was coming from, take responsibility, and apologize for interrupting her. Instead, Emma said: "I didn't agree with what you were saying and felt it was important to voice my opinion before you went further."

Kate didn't hear what she wanted to, but because she had prepared for this possible scenario she said: *"Look, I realize that you wouldn't do that on purpose to upset me."* (**understanding**)

Emma responded: "Of course I wouldn't do that to upset you. I didn't know if I'd have the opportunity to voice my opinion if I didn't speak up right away."

Kate felt it was important to add a phrase of apology to keep Emma from becoming defensive, so she immediately added: *"I apologize if this seems trivial."* (**apology**)

Emma did not back down: "Yeah, I do think it's trivial."

Kate knew that if she wanted Emma's behavior to stop, she'd need to continue the conversation. She also knew, by Emma's demeanor, that she needed to be assertive, yet remain calm. "To me it wasn't trivial. Do you have a few minutes now? *I'd like to talk this over and find an agreeable solution.* (**compromise**) Let's go into the conference room where we can talk in private."

Kate sensed that Emma felt uncomfortable and that she'd need to tread lightly. After closing the door, she began: *"Why don't we try to look at the situation from each other's viewpoint? That may help us find a solution."* (**compromise**)

"Okay, sure," Emma said. "You don't like me disagreeing with you, and I felt it was important to voice my opinion."

"That's not what bothered me. *I understand that we're not always going to agree.* (**understanding**) What bothered me was that you interrupted me during the middle of my presentation and it really threw me off track. *I would have appreciated if you waited until I was done speaking to voice your disagreement.*" (**compromise**)

"I'm sorry if I threw you off track. That would have bothered me too. It's just that I didn't know if I'd have the chance if I waited. In another meeting I did wait and, when you finished speaking, the discussion changed direction and I wasn't able to make my point."

"*Oh, I can understand how frustrating that must have been.* (**understanding**) *How does this sound? From now on, if you'll allow me to finish my presentation without interrupting, I'll see to it that we don't move on to another topic before asking if anyone would like to add something. That way, you'll be able to voice your opinion.*" (**compromise**)

"That works for me."

Kate felt that Emma now understood her position and agreed with her proposed solution. Then she restated the resolution: "*Now I have a better understanding of your viewpoint. After finishing any future presentations, I'll make sure you get a chance to speak up, even if it is to disagree with me!*" (**resolution**) They laughed and both felt good that they were able to resolve the problem.

Then Kate added: "*"I'm so glad we talked this out. I value our working relationship and wouldn't want anything to detract from that.*" (**reconciliation**)

Why This Works

When you compare the two conversations, you probably knew from the way in which Kate began the first conversation that it was going to head downhill quickly. In the second scenario, even though Kate was upset about what happened, she took time to think about the best way to approach Emma. She also played through different conversation scenarios in her mind so that she wouldn't be caught off guard.

She opened with an "I" phrase, which sounded much better than opening with a "you" phrase blaming Emma for interrupting her. By offering phrases of understanding, Kate demonstrated that she was open to hearing Emma's point of view. Kate also offered a phrase of apology, hoping that would help Emma empathize with her. Then, throughout their conversation, Kate interjected phrases of compromise to continue the dialogue. When Emma mentioned that on a previous occasion she wasn't able to voice her opinion, Kate had an *aha* moment. She was able to see the situation from Emma's perspective and understood how not being able to speak up made her feel. Kate then voiced a phrase of understanding, and they reached an agreement that in the future Emma would hold her comments and Kate would make sure that she allowed time for discussion. A phrase of resolution followed by a phrase of reconciliation ended the conversation on a positive note.

2

Actions That Enhance Powerful Phrases

You might think communication is just the words you speak, but it involves much more than words. Your nonverbal actions actually communicate more than what you say. That's because your words convey your message, but your actions convey the feelings and emotions behind it. Nonverbal communication is the actions you take as you speak and listen. If used effectively, these actions enhance your powerful phrases.

Nonverbal communication is comprised of body language, facial expressions, voice tone, and level of assertiveness. Body language includes your stance, posture, arm-and-hand movements, and gestures. Facial expressions are your mouth, eye, and eyebrow movements. Tone of voice, though verbal in nature, is considered a nonverbal action because your tone communicates what you're feeling. Assertiveness is reflected outward by acting confidently and with self-assurance. Even when you think before you speak and choose your words wisely, if your nonverbal actions don't agree with your verbal message, it can confuse the other person, who's more likely to assess the message based on your nonverbal actions than on what you said.

Your nonverbal actions have a direct affect on how others view you. They can increase your ability to get along and communicate well with your peers and boss or create a problem between you and another person. Just going about your daily work routine may cause someone to view you negatively. Let's say that you usually greet your coworkers with a facial expression that projects a lack of interest, you don't make eye contact when you speak to others, you speak in a tone tinged with boredom, and you never speak up or defend yourself. It's likely your coworkers will keep you at arm's length or take advantage of you. However, you can learn to use nonverbal actions to your advantage. Let's say that you always maintain a friendly facial expression, make eye contact when conversing, use a calm and nonthreatening tone, and speak assertively when explaining your actions. Then it's likely that others will view you as friendly, open, confident, and self-assured.

Whenever you communicate, it's important that your actions match your words, but especially so when resolving a problem. As you read this chapter, practice the nonverbal actions you're learning so that they become natural rather than forced. When you present yourself well through your body language, facial expressions, voice tone, and assertive actions, you enhance the message you're voicing. And when you're comfortable matching your actions with your words in regular conversations, you'll find it easier to control your actions when confronting a coworker in a conflict resolution conversation.

Nonverbal actions can also be helpful in determining other people's feelings and emotions. For example, if you begin a conflict resolution dialogue with a coworker by saying: *"I was surprised that you took credit for creating a problem-solving team when I was the one who approached you about it,"* and your coworker responds by saying: "I'm sorry. I didn't realize I did that," it sounds as though your coworker is taking responsibility. But if, as your coworker delivers these words, he gets an arrogant look on his face, gestures as if he doesn't know what you're talking about, and speaks in a disrespectful tone, your understanding of the message changes completely, doesn't it?

As you see, actions play an important role in all communication. The better you understand your own actions, the better you'll be able to understand other people's actions. This will enable you to communicate more effectively and establish constructive and productive dialogues.

Resolving Conflict: The Wrong Way

Andrew and his coworker, James, have been working on a project to develop a new program to increase sales revenue in their department. They were slated to present their interim report to the vice president of marketing during yesterday's staff meeting. Andrew and James had spent a lot of time practicing their joint presentation and decided that each would speak about different key aspects of their proposal. James volunteered to go first and provide an overview of their project. Andrew waited for his turn to present the details, but James continued speaking and handled the entire presentation. Andrew's dismay turned to feelings of betrayal when James took most of the credit for the project, merely mentioning that Andrew helped and thanking him for his contributions. Because it wouldn't have looked professional to interrupt James, Andrew sat through the presentation in stunned silence. By the end of the presentation, he was seething but managed to keep a neutral facial expression.

After the meeting, Andrew was so angry he couldn't take it anymore. He thought first before approaching James and planned what he wanted to say: *"I was really stunned that you handled the entire presentation. That wasn't how we practiced it, and it made me look like I hadn't contributed as much as you."* (**"I" phrase**) But Andrew hadn't given any thought to how he'd control his emotions. He spoke in an angry tone, crossed his arms in front of his body, and the neutral expression he was able to maintain during the meeting turned to an indignant glare.

James replied: "I'm sorry. It's just that once I got going it didn't seem appropriate to break up the presentation."

Andrew paid close attention to James's actions when he spoke. James raised his eyebrows, shook his head casually, shrugged his shoulders, and looked beyond Andrew rather than making make eye contact. His tone was dismissive, which made Andrew even angrier. Clearly, James didn't feel sorry at all, but only said the words to appease Andrew.

Andrew blurted out sarcastically: "Well, when it's time to give the final presentation I'll handle it. And I'll be sure to thank you for your help, just like you thanked me for helping you."

James shrugged his shoulders and said: "Hey, why don't you man up? It was only the interim presentation, not a big deal."

Andrew retorted: "Not a big deal? Just wait until the final presentation. Then you can decide how big a deal it is."

Why This Doesn't Work

Andrew had a right to be upset when James controlled the presentation and took credit for the project. And, although Andrew thought about how to approach James to avoid this scenario when they gave the final presentation, he sent James a negative message by beginning his conversation, crossing his arms in front of his body and using an angry tone. As a result, James responded dismissively. Although the right words were spoken, both men's actions conveyed their true feelings. When James trivialized the situation, Andrew's tone turned to sarcasm and the conversation quickly degraded to a derogatory banter between the coworkers. Unless they're able to resolve this conflict in a more productive manner, it's going to be extremely tough for them to work cohesively, complete this project, and plan for their final presentation.

Something to Think About

When you're planning how to begin your conflict resolution conversation, practice your opening statement in a mirror to be sure your actions agree with your powerful phrases. And, it's always a good idea to calm down before approaching your coworker.

Body Language

Anytime you're communicating, it's important to be aware of your body language because your posture, stance, movements, and gestures send very clear signals. How you stand or sit and what you do with your hands provide clues to what you're feeling and what you're thinking. They even reveal what you think of yourself. Whether you stand or sit up straight or slump, you send a message. Whether you allow your hands to fall naturally at your sides or fidget with them, you send a message. And, whether you use controlled gestures to enhance your message or gesture exaggeratedly, you send a message.

In addition, body language is affected by a person's level of comfort when it comes to proximity and personal space. Whenever someone gets too close and starts invading our space, our discomfort increases instantly. Once someone enters it, a person's body language communicates exactly what he or she is feeling. When your space is invaded, you're likely to back up, distance yourself from the invader, and reclaim your personal space before feeling comfortable continuing the conversation. So always be mindful of other people's personal space. If you notice that a person with whom you're speaking is continually leaning back or stepping away, it's time to back off.

In casual or normal conversations, body language should be easy to control once you form good habits. But when your emotions are heightened, your body language is likely to be more exaggerated. You may move around more than normal. You may cross your arms in front of you as a defensive signal. You may point your finger at the person or gesture wildly. And, you may move into someone's personal space. That's why practicing your body language actions before you enter into a conflict resolution conversation will help you stay mindful of the image you're projecting.

Sample Body Language

If you want to be viewed as confident, competent, capable, composed, and comfortable in your surroundings, form the following habits:

- Stand or sit up straight.
- Hold your head high.
- Maintain good posture.
- Relax your shoulders.
- Keep a relaxed stance by standing with equal weight on both feet.
- Allow your hands to fall naturally at your sides or fold them in front of you in a relaxed position.
- Keep your hands out of your pockets.
- Try not to fidget.
- Use controlled gestures to enhance your message, allowing them to flow naturally.
- Stand about two to four feet from the other person.

Reading Other People's Body Language

Watch for these actions in other people:

- Stooped shoulders, which may signal a lack of confidence.

- Fidgeting with hands, which may signal nervousness or agitation.
- Hands on hips, which may be a sign of impatience or aggression.
- Arms crossed in front of the body, which could mean the person is defensive or frustrated.
- Wild gesturing, which may be a sign of anger, excitement, or agitation.
- Backing up, which probably means that you're invading their personal space.

If you notice any of these signals, maintain a relaxed demeanor and stay calm. Doing so may help the other person calm down.

Incorporating Body Language

Even though Andrew was angry, he thought about what he wanted to say to James. He also knew it was important to present himself in a composed manner so that his message would be understood as intended.

When he saw James, he said: *"I was really stunned that you handled the entire presentation. That wasn't how we practiced it, and it made me look like I hadn't contributed as much as you."* (**"I" phrase**) As he spoke, Andrew maintained a confident demeanor. He held his head high, maintained good posture, kept his hands by his sides, and did not fidget or gesture.

Something to Think About

Touch is another component of body language. Putting your arm around someone, touching someone's arm, or patting someone on the back may enhance the message you're sending, but it can also detract from it. Make sure you know the other person well enough to know that touch is welcomed; otherwise, keep your hands to yourself.

Facial Expressions

Your face can easily be a snapshot of what you're feeling, especially if you're angry, upset, or emotional about a situation. Facial expressions and eye and eyebrow movements can be powerful communication tools when used to complete the message you're vocalizing. But our facial expressions often are automatic responses to what we're feeling. Whether we're happy or sad, it's going to show. And, when we're angry or upset, it's natural to project those feelings outward by scowling, furrowing our brows, narrowing our eyes, and pursing our lips. The good news is that with practice you'll avoid wearing your emotions on your face. You can form positive habits and use facial expressions to your advantage, without looking stone faced. Rather, you can come across as concerned, sincere, interested, and calm. When you control your facial expressions, your listener is apt to be more open to the message you're delivering. Let's face it: no one wants to launch into a conversation with an angry-looking coworker!

In addition to controlling your facial expression, learn to smile frequently. A smile is one of the most positive and uplifting body language messages you can send, even when confronting someone about a problem. A sincere smile shows that you're open, willing to listen to the other person, and interested in talking through the situation. If you can't smile about a situation that's upset or angered you, then just turning your mouth muscles slightly upward projects a pleasant expression.

Eye contact is another important component of facial expressions, but it can be a tough habit to form. When you begin any conversation, make a conscious effort to look directly at the other person's eyes. Then maintain eye contact that's comfortable, glancing away and bringing your focus back occasionally so that you don't look as though you're glaring. Along with eye contact, your eyebrow movement can enhance or detract from your message. Raised eyebrows convey interest, enthusiasm, shock, or excitement. Furrowed brows may signal concern, confusion, or anger. Use your eyebrows to your advantage, but don't overdo it by continually raising or furrowing your eyebrows or the other person is likely to focus more on why you're doing that than on listening to your message.

Sample Facial Expressions

To enhance the body language actions you learned, complete the image you want to project by becoming comfortable doing the following:

- Calm down and maintain a concerned and sincere expression rather than an angry scowl if you're feeling angry or upset.
- Hold your head up straight rather than lowering it to the floor or tilting it to one side.
- Smile when appropriate.
- Turn the ends of your mouth upward slightly to convey friendliness when you want to keep a neutral expression.
- Maintain eye contact, but not to the degree that you appear to be staring. Shift your gaze away occasionally.
- Use your eyebrows once in a while to enhance your message. Raise them to show interest or excitement. Furrow them to convey concern or confusion.
- Nod from time to time to show that you're actively listening.

Reading Other People's Facial Expressions

Look for the following facial expressions that provide clues to a person's emotional state:

- Lowering the head and looking downward, which could mean the person is ashamed or trying to avoid you.

- Tilting the head to one side, which could signal confusion or a challenge to what you're saying.

- Pursing lips or downturning the mouth, which can be signs of anger, distrust, or sadness.

- Looking past you, or down, or up, which may signal discomfort, guilt, distrust, or dishonesty.

- Frequent blinking, which is often a signal of discomfort or distress.

- Furrowing brows, which may signal anger, agitation, or confusion.

- Raising brows, which may signal enthusiasm, surprise, amazement, or disbelief.

Incorporating Facial Expressions

When Andrew saw James, he said: *"I was really stunned that you handled the entire presentation. That wasn't how we practiced it, and it made me look like I hadn't contributed as much as you."* (**"I" phrase**) As he spoke, he held his head up high, maintained good posture, kept his hands by his sides, and did not fidget or gesture. He made eye contact with James, his facial expression showed concern, and he smiled slightly to show sincerity.

Tone of Voice

Voice tone is also considered a nonverbal action because how you say something truly is more important that what you're saying. For example, if you open a conversation with an "I" phrase, such as: *"I need to talk to you about something,"* the meaning will be understood by your tone, which, conveys how you feel. It's important that your tone conveys the correct message. So, when you begin a conflict resolution conversation by saying, *"I need to talk to you about something,"* speaking in a neutral or concerned tone is your best bet to receive a positive response.

In addition to your tone, your message is affected by how loudly and how fast you speak. If you're trying to remain calm when you feel upset about something, speaking softly and slowly will actually help you calm down. Further, the sounds you make when listening can show whether you understand, agree with, or are confused by the message. When you say "ahh," "hmm," "oh," or "mhmm," it shows that you're up to speed with the conversation. When you utter "hmm?" or "oh?," it signals you're confused or don't agree with what you're hearing.

Something to Think About

Some people have formed the habit of using up-speak—ending every sentence by raising voice pitch—in their voice tone, as if they're asking a question. If you do this, break the habit. It really serves no purpose.

Sample Tone of Voice

To communicate effectively, it's important to match your voice tone to your emotions, but it's also important to control your voice tone when resolving conflict. For example:

- When beginning your conversation, speak in a tone that sounds professional and nonthreatening.
- Throughout your conversation, use your tone to enhance your message by showing concern and empathy.
- If you notice that your tone is reflecting that you're feeling upset or confused about a situation, try to also show that you're interested in working together toward a positive solution.

Reading Other People's Tone of Voice

Listen to how the other person is speaking to you to pick up clues to their emotions.

- If the person sounds angry, speak softly and calmly.
- If the person sounds confused, provide more details to explain your position.
- If the person sounds guilty or embarrassed, smile sympathetically and say something to ease his or her discomfort.
- If the person sounds dismissive, speak in a concerned tone and state why you feel the way you do.
- If the person is speaking quickly or loudly, control your voice by speaking slowly and softly, as that may help the other person calm down.

Incorporating Tone of Voice Actions

When Andrew saw James, he said: *"I was really stunned that you handled the entire presentation. That wasn't how we practiced it, and it made me look like I hadn't contributed as much as you."* (**"I" phrase**) As he spoke, he held his head up high, maintained good posture, kept his hands by his sides, and did not fidget or gesture. He made eye contact with James, his facial expression showed concern, and he smiled slightly to show sincerity. He began the conversation by speaking in a neutral tone, but changed to a concerned tone when he said that wasn't how they practiced the presentation.

Assertiveness

Assertiveness is a state of mind that's projected outward as confidence and self-assurance. Although it is sometimes confused with aggressiveness, there's a distinct difference between the two. Assertiveness means saying what's on your mind, carefully choosing your words, matching your actions to what you're saying, and being respectful toward the other person. Aggressiveness means saying what's on your mind when it comes to mind, giving no thought as to how you're going to present yourself, and ignoring the nonverbal signals you send. If you act aggressively, you'll likely come across as angry, arrogant, bossy, or egotistical. Therefore, when you want to resolve conflict, project assertiveness by acting confidently and self-assuredly. The other person is then more likely to listen to you.

Assertiveness is an important life skill to develop. It shows that you care enough to stand up for yourself constructively and respectfully. However, most people aren't born assertive; it's a learned skill. To gain confidence when approaching another person, learn to think through a situation before speaking, view the situation from the other person's perspective, and plan how you want to present yourself. To be assertive, you need to speak and act confidently. When you practice doing that, your comfort level will grow until assertiveness becomes part of your persona.

Something to Think About

Pay attention to the people around you who are assertive. Watch how they present themselves and learn the positive techniques that will help you become more assertive.

Sample Assertiveness

Assertiveness is reflected outward through the following actions:

- Speaking with confidence.
- Expressing your views clearly.

- Speaking objectively.
- Staying calm.
- Controlling your emotions when stating your position.
- Apologizing no more than necessary.
- Refusing to back down or allow someone to verbally bully you.
- Showing respect and consideration toward the other person.

Reading Other People's Level of Assertiveness

Knowing how to read the other person's level of assertiveness will enhance your ability to work through a problem.

- If the person immediately backs down, show compassion. Try to draw them back into the conversation so that you may work toward a win–win solution. Never take advantage of a person who isn't assertive.

- If the person becomes angry or aggressive, remain calm. Speak in a soft, controlled voice. It may help to address that person's emotions by saying something like: "I understand that you're angry about this. Let's talk it out and find a solution we both agree to." By remaining calm and speaking softly, you'll help the other person calm down.

Incorporating Assertiveness

When Andrew saw James, he said: *"I was really stunned that you handled the entire presentation. That wasn't how we practiced it, and it made me look like I hadn't contributed as much as you."* **("I" phrase)** As he spoke, he held his head up high, maintained good posture, kept his hands by his sides, and did not fidget or gesture. He made eye contact with James, his facial expression showed concern, and he smiled slightly to show sincerity. He began the conversation by speaking confidently and assertively using a neutral tone, but changed to a concerned tone when he said that wasn't how they practiced the presentation.

Resolving Conflict: The Right Way

Andrew and his coworker, James, have been working on a project to develop a new program to increase sales revenue in their department. They were slated to present their interim report to the vice president of marketing during yesterday's staff meeting. Andrew and James had spent a lot of time practicing their joint presentation and decided that each would speak about different the key aspects of their proposal. James volunteered to go first part and provide an overview of their project. Andrew awaited for his turn to present the details, but James continued speaking and handled the entire presentation. Andrew's dismay turned to feelings of betrayal when James took most of the credit for the project, merely mentioning that Andrew helped and thanking him for his contributions. Because it wouldn't have looked professional to interrupt James, Andrew sat through the presentation in stunned silence. By the end of the presentation he was seething but managed to keep a neutral facial expression.

When Andrew saw James, he said: *"I was really stunned that you handled the entire presentation. That wasn't how we practiced it, and it made me look like I hadn't contributed as much as you."* (**"I" phrase**) As he spoke, he held his head up high, maintained good posture, kept his hands by his sides, and did not fidget or gesture. He made eye contact with James, his facial expression showed concern, and he smiled slightly to show sincerity. He began the conversation by speaking assertively using a neutral tone, but changed to a concerned tone when he said that wasn't how they practiced the presentation.

James replied: "I'm sorry. It's just that once I got going it didn't seem appropriate to break up the presentation."

Andrew paid close attention to James's actions when he spoke. James raised his eyebrows, shook his head glibly, shrugged his shoulders, looked beyond Andrew rather than making make eye contact, and used a dismissive tone. Clearly, James didn't feel sorry at all, but only said the words to appease Andrew.

Andrew thought that James might respond in this manner, but he did not back down or lose his confidence. He maintained his relaxed stance, continued to make eye contact, and spoke in a concerned tone. *"I can understand that during the presentation you might have felt that way.* **(understanding)** But, since we both contributed equally throughout this project, *I would have appreciated being able to take part in the presentation."* **("I" phrase)** Andrew paused to give James a chance to respond, still paying close attention to his nonverbal actions.

James crossed his arms in front of his body and looked down. He shrugged his shoulders and replied: "Well, what can I say? What's done is done."

Andrew was dismayed that James didn't seem to understand how he felt during the presentation, but it was important that they resolve the issue. "Yes, you're right, what's done is done. *But I'd like to talk this out so we can agree on how to handle the next presentation."* **(compromise)**

James relaxed his stance, dropping his hands to his sides. "Sure."

Andrew then reiterated: *"I hope you can look at this from my point of view.* Let's say that I started the presentation and when it was your turn to speak, I continued and handled the entire presentation. When you did that to me, *I really felt devalued."* **("I" phrase)**

James furrowed his brows and nodded. "You're right. I wouldn't have liked that done to me. Hey man, I'm really sorry. I guess I just got caught up in the excitement of all the work we put into this."

"I totally see where that could happen. **(understanding)** *During the next presentation, I'd like to speak first. And I promise that I'll turn it over to you when it's your turn. How does that sound?"* **(compromise)**

"I agree. And I wouldn't blame you if you decided to handle it all." He laughed. Andrew smiled warmly.

"No, a deal's a deal. I'll speak first but we'll each handle a portion of the presentation." They shook hands and then Andrew added: *"I'm glad we talked about this."* (**resolution**)

James nodded and smiled.

Andrew added: *"We've worked so well up to this point I wouldn't want anything to cause a rift between us."* (**reconciliation**)

Why This Works

When Andrew thought about how to confront James, he also thought about his actions. He knew James was a headstrong person who wasn't likely to take responsibility for what he did, so Andrew wanted to make sure he spoke and acted assertively. As he rehearsed what he wanted to say, he also practiced his body language and facial expressions. He wanted to look relaxed yet confident and be sure he maintained eye contact.

Because he also paid close attention to James's actions, Andrew discerned that as soon as the conversation began, James assumed a defensive pose. So, when James dismissively shrugged his shoulders and replied, "what's done is done," Andrew didn't back down. Instead, he assertively responded with a phrase of compromise. The two men were then able to continue their dialogue in a constructive manner, with Andrew taking the lead and offering phrases of compromise, resolution, and reconciliation. Because Andrew was assertive and used his nonverbal actions to enhance his message, the two men were able to come to an agreement and it's likely that he and James will be able to plan the next presentation without further problems.

Effective Conflict Resolution = Strengthened Work Relationships

3

Five Steps to Effective Conflict Resolution

P eople don't always get along. Conflicts happen. It's how you deal with conflict that can strengthen relationships, negatively affect relationships, or sever them completely. When two or more people disagree, the issue must be addressed before it escalates out of control. It's important to note that conflict is a natural component in any relationship; therefore, viewing every conflict as an opportunity to grow and strengthen the relationship will help you look for successful ways to work through the problem. That's accomplished by communicating openly, understanding the other person's point of view, and working toward a solution that's agreeable to all parties. Good resolution discussion clears up confusion, channels positive energy, boosts confidence, helps people move forward, and ultimately strengthens relationships.

Keeping your work relationships strong may be easy to achieve when things are running smoothly, but what happens when there's a problem? Conflicts can quickly erode even the closest relationships and often arise when someone feels slighted, left out of the loop, or unfairly treated. Causes may include poor communication, a misunderstanding, the occurrence of many changes, a disagreement between people, or a personality clash. Conflicts are also common in high-producing teams in which people are creative and passionate about their work. Basically, any time people view a situation from different perspectives, conflicts can arise.

However, conflict is not all bad. Without it, people can become bored, complacent, or stagnant. When every conflict is viewed as an opportunity, you'll look for resolutions that allow for growth and development. Effective conflict resolution gets people back on track, opens the door to creative thought processes, and paves the way to open, honest, and effective communication.

When you're vigilant and on the lookout for problems, you can work to resolve issues when they're still manageable. Become an active observer and communicator. Stay involved and look for things that seem askew. Be aware of coworkers who suddenly become negative, quiet, agitated, or upset, as these are often signs of conflict. Watch for signs that you and your boss aren't communicating effectively. Even if you're unaware of a problem, but notice that a coworker or your boss is acting in a way that indicates a conflict, ask what's going on, because something likely is.

For every problem, someone must take ownership of the issue and work to resolve it. If you're that someone, whether the issue is between you and another person or you're responsible for mediating conflict between others, there's another element to conflict resolution: the time factor. Once you're aware of a problem, you don't have the luxury of time to see how it'll play out.

Remaining calm and in control when dealing with conflict is essential. If the issue doesn't directly involve you, it should be easy to stay composed. But what happens when you are involved? It's going to be much more difficult to control your emotions, but maintaining self-control and objectivity is paramount. If you find it difficult to stay calm, take some deep breaths to help slow your racing heart. Better yet, make it a rule to always take time to fully think through a situation and calm down before entering into a discussion. Any time you're having a hard time controlling your emotions during a discussion, postpone it to a later time. It's better to walk away than lose control.

The bottom line is that you can effectively deal with conflict when you take the time to learn and practice the five-step process presented in this chapter. At first, you'll most likely feel uncomfortable confronting conflict. You'll stumble and make mistakes. But when you recognize these skills have begun to yield positive outcomes, you'll become more comfortable in dealing with a minor disagreement with a coworker or resolving a major problem that affects a group of people. As you become more comfortable, your confidence will grow. As your confidence grows, your coworkers and boss will see that you're a person of action who seeks solutions and looks for the best outcomes.

Resolving Conflict: The Wrong Way

Dave and his coworkers, Tanya, Chad, and Angela, are a cohesive, close-knit team. In the past, whenever a problem's come up, they've been able to work through it. But then Diana, Dave's boss, asked him to take over as team leader while she'll be out on a one-month maternity leave. Even though Dave is the newest member of the team, he felt proud that she chose him. He was confident that her decision was based on his demonstration of strong leadership skills, his knowledge of the job duties, and his role as the go-to person on the team.

As soon as his boss made the announcement, Dave immediately noticed a subtle change in his coworkers. During the meeting, Tanya looked down and didn't speak. Chad's facial expression became solemn and, as he nodded his head slowly, he glanced at Angela, who raised her eyebrows and didn't look too happy either. After the meeting, Dave observed his coworkers huddled closely together. When he walked up to them, they stopped their conversation midsentence. Dave knew they were upset because he was chosen. He felt hurt that they weren't happy for him, but because they had always worked well together, he assumed they'd get over whatever negative feelings they were experiencing.

However, that didn't happen. After a week, his coworkers barely acknowledged him. When Dave asked Chad to take over a project that he'd been working on, Chad took the paperwork and threw it onto his desk. Dave didn't know what to make of Chad's reaction so he said: "Hey Chad, if it's too much for you to handle, I'll find a way to do it."

Chad shrugged his shoulders and said nothing, so Dave took the project back. He figured everyone was upset at having to do additional work. Even though he knew it would be a hardship for him, Dave didn't want to make waves, so he vowed to handle his workload plus Diana's. He wasn't happy with how his coworkers seemed to turn against him, but he didn't want to say anything that might upset them more.

Why This Doesn't Work

When Dave walked up to his coworkers who were huddled together, he knew something was wrong. He used the wrong approach by not dealing directly with the problem and hoping that things would smooth out by themselves over time. Remember that not confronting any sort of conflict will not make the problem go away. Rather, it makes the problem fester and grow. After the first week that his coworkers were barely civil to him, Dave should have discussed the problem with them. His decision to complete his work as well as to take care of Diana's responsibilities placed a needless hardship on him and made him look weak in his coworker's eyes. Because they had been a cohesive team, talking it out would have proved more beneficial for the team.

Step 1: Think First

When you're embroiled in a conflict, it may be tough to take time to think about the issue, but such thought is essential to help you look at the issue objectively. When you keep your objectivity, you can explore other perspectives, which may even change your own. You do that by staying focused on the issue rather than on the person. Before assuming that's someone's done something to you on purpose or is out to get you, take a step back, rein in your emotions, and look at the situation from all angles. This may help you gain an understanding of the person's intentions. Even if you still can't explain why the person acted as he or she did, taking the time to calm down and think rationally will put you in a better position to effectively discuss the problem.

You may be drawn into situations in which you aren't personally involved in the conflict, but are asked to take sides. You can easily fall into the trap of siding with one person and becoming emotionally involved, especially if it's a friend or close coworker. Even though your tendency is to agree with your friend, try not to. Take time to think through the situation before acting. Don't readily assume that the other person is at fault. Maintain your objectivity and help your coworker calm down and think through the situation from all perspectives. When you do that consistently, others will see you as someone who doesn't jump to conclusions and who's able to objectify conflicts rather than pass judgment.

Key Points

Practice the following to help you think first:

- Never act or speak before you think.
- Take time to calm down and control your emotions.
- Look at the situation from all perspectives.

- Stay objective when thinking about the conflict.
- Focus on the problem, not the person.
- Think through your conversation, along with likely responses.
- Refrain from taking sides in other people's problems.
- Try to help the other person objectify the situation, rather than make judgments.

Taking Time to Think About a Conflict

Dave and his coworkers, Tanya, Chad, and Angela are a cohesive, close-knit team. In the past, whenever a problem's come up they've been able to work through it. But then Diana, Dave's boss, asked him to take over as team leader while she'll be out on a one-month maternity leave. Even though Dave is the newest member of the team, he felt proud that she chose him. He was confident that her decision was based on his demonstration of strong leadership skills, his knowledge of the job duties, and his role as the go-to person on the team.

As soon as his boss made the announcement, Dave noticed a subtle change in his coworkers. During the meeting, Tanya looked down and didn't speak. Chad's facial expression became solemn and, as he nodded his head slowly, he glanced at Angela, who raised her eyebrows and didn't look too happy either. After the meeting, Dave observed his co-workers huddled closely together. When he walked up to them, they stopped their conversation midsentence. Dave knew they were upset because he was chosen. He felt hurt that they weren't happy for him, but he knew that if wanted the team to continue to operate efficiently and effectively, he needed to talk with his team members and resolve the problem before it got out of hand.

First, he thought about how to proceed by evaluating each person's personality and how he or she was likely to respond. He kept his objectivity as he played out different scenarios. Then, he planned how to open the discussion and how he'd work through the process to resolve the problem.

Step 2: Gain a Better Understanding

After reining in your emotions and looking at the situation from the other person's viewpoint, you may have a better understanding of what caused the situation and decide it really isn't a problem after all. If this is not the case, before drawing conclusions or making decisions, you need to talk with the other person about the situation. This should increase your understanding of the person's intent. When you address the issue by asking questions to uncover additional facts, you'll be in a better position to decide how to proceed with your conversation.

If you're the one taking ownership to resolve a conflict between others, the best approach to gaining a better understanding is to get the involved parties together and allow each person to tell his or her version of the story. Encourage everyone to use "I" phrases, such as: *I noticed...*, *I felt...*, or *From my perspective....* Doing this keeps the discussion on a nonjudgmental basis and the participants won't feel the need to become defensive.

Still, there's always the chance that people will become defensive or emotional when talking about the conflict. If this happens, pay close attention to the nonverbal cues and listen carefully to the message being sent. Is the person hurt, angry, or embarrassed? What's the message behind the words? Maintain eye contact, and show concern in your facial expressions, but don't frown, laugh, act nonchalant, or send improper messages. Before responding, allow the person to vent and try not to interrupt. Listen respectfully, as this will often help someone who's angry to calm down. No matter how emotional someone else becomes, when it's your turn to respond, be patient, be calm, and stay in control of your emotions.

If, at any time, someone appears to be losing control, keep your composure and speak in a calm, soft voice. Assure the person you're simply trying to gain a better understanding. Focus on the behavior and offer an assurance that you want to resolve the problem. Say something like: *"I'm trying to find out why this happened so we can resolve the issue. I can see that you're getting upset. Why don't we take a few minutes to calm down and then we can discuss the issue. Let's take a walk to the break room and get a cup of coffee."*

Something to Think About

Timing is critical. Before launching into a discussion, make sure it's a good time, and, if it isn't, schedule a time when everyone can get together. You may also consider delaying a meeting if people are emotional and, when you do meet, choose a private place.

Key Points

Practice the following when gaining a better understanding:

- Never draw conclusions before first speaking to the other person.
- Question the other person in an objective and respectful manner.
- Carefully listen to the response so that you gain an understanding of how the other person views the issue.
- If more than two people are involved, get everyone together and allow each person to tell his or her version of the situation.
- Encourage everyone to use "I phrases" when explaining.
- If someone becomes emotional, pay attention to the nonverbal clues behind the message.
- Listen carefully, and avoid interrupting.

- When it's your turn to respond, control your emotions.
- If someone becomes upset or starts losing control of his or her emotions, acknowledge and offer an assurance. Defer your discussion until the person has had time to calm down.

Gaining a Better Understanding of the Situation

Dave told everyone he wanted to talk with them and called the team together in the conference room. He began: "When Diana made the announcement that I'd be taking over as team leader, *I felt that you were bothered by that decision, and I think we need to talk about this so we don't lose the closeness we've developed as a team*." (**"I" phrase, compromise**)

"It's important for us to be honest with each other," he continued, "so I'd like everyone to truthfully say how you feel about me being team leader."

No one spoke up, so Dave said: "Chad, will you start? Tell me how you felt when Diana made the announcement."

Chad shifted uncomfortably in his seat and responded: "Even though you're the newest member on the team, I understand why Diana chose you. What bothered me is that it isn't fair that the three of us are now going to have to do our work plus yours."

Dave nodded. *"I understand that."* (**understanding**) "Angela?"

"At first, part of me felt it should have gone by seniority. Tanya's been here the longest. But that's not what bothered me the most. I agree with Chad. We've all got our plates full now. How are we supposed to take on more work?"

Dave turned to Tanya. "Do you agree with that?"

"Well, I don't agree that just because I've been here the longest I should have been chosen," Tanya replied. "I think Diana made the right call when she picked you because you're the strongest member of our team. What bothered me is what Chad and Angela said. How are three people supposed to do the work of four?"

Step 3: Define the Problem

When all the involved parties have expressed their views about the situation and you feel confident that you have a good understanding, you'll be able to define the problem by assertively stating how you view the issue. Defining the problem involves saying "This is how I see it . . ." and then giving others the opportunity to express how they see it. By acknowledging everyone's point of view in an objective manner, you show that you respect everyone's opinion. You'll clear up any confusion and ensure that everyone has had the opportunity to express and agree on the definition of the problem. If you discover that someone hasn't spoken up, encourage that person by saying: "What's your take on this, Shannon?"

Defining the problem is necessary before you can find an agreeable solution. After recapping everyone's take on the issue, check if someone is confused or doesn't agree with what you're saying. If necessary, go back a step and allow that person to present his or her side again to clear up any misunderstandings. What's important is to ensure that you have everyone's input and that you define the problem before moving on to the next step.

Key Points

Practice the following when defining the problem:

- When you feel you have enough information, restate the problem from your viewpoint. Then ask others how they view the problem.
- Say something like: "I see it this way.... How do you see it?"

- Before you move on to find a workable solution, everyone must agree on how the problem is defined.

Defining the Problem to Clarify the Points of View

Dave took a moment to plan his response. Then he said: "Thanks for your input. I appreciate that you're supportive that I'll be team leader. I also appreciate your concern as to how the work's going to get done. Is that how all of you see it?"

He paid attention to their nonverbal signals as they each nodded in agreement. They seemed a little more relaxed now that Dave had defined the problem.

"*I certainly understand where you're coming from.* (**understanding**) I assure you that I've already thought about that, and it concerns me too. I feel strongly that we're going to resolve this issue so that we can all work together. Ultimately, when Diana comes back from maternity leave, I want her to see that we're the same close-knit team we've always been."

Step 4: Offer Your Best Solution

You began your discussion by thinking about the situation in order to keep an open mind and take an objective approach. You asked questions, listened to answers, and responded appropriately in an effort to better understand the issue. You defined the problem by stating everyone's viewpoint and gained agreement from the involved parties as to how they view the problem. Now it's time to work toward an agreeable solution. Begin by offering your best solution and then allow others to either agree or offer an alternative. Make sure that you remain flexible and cooperative if someone disagrees with your proposed solution. Encourage cooperation among the involved parties. When people are willing to cooperate, it's a productive way to resolve the conflict; otherwise the problem is likely to flare up in the future.

When you offer your solution, encourage discussion and keep the focus on the purpose of your meeting: to find the best solution that everyone can buy into. This isn't the place to decide who's right and who's wrong. It may help to state this: "Let's be respectful of everyone's viewpoints. It's important that we remain flexible, cooperate, and be able to compromise." If you feel the discussion starts heading toward a blame game, politely interrupt and assertively say that it isn't the purpose to assign blame, but rather to find a solution everyone can agree to. After everyone's contributed, objectively analyze the consequences of each proposal. That will keep everyone focused on the issue at hand and keep the discussion solution oriented.

Keep in mind that most of your conflicts are likely to involve you and one other person rather than a group. Thus, offer your best solution and ask the other person if he or she agrees. If not, encourage the other person to offer another solution and be prepared to discuss what's best.

During this step, respect differences and varying viewpoints. Try to find something on which you can agree, as this will move you closer to resolution. Pay attention to nonverbal cues, which can help you figure out what the other person is looking to gain from the resolution. If you can't agree, be prepared to give a little by offering a compromise. When you show that you're willing to compromise, the other person will be more open to giving a little as well, which will help you continue negotiating to an agreeable end result.

If your role is to facilitate the discussion and guide others to reach an agreement, maintain your objectivity, but understand that you may be pulled into other people's emotions. When you're listening, incorporate positive words into your comments, such as "That sounds like it'll work," "I can see you're all trying hard to find a solution," or "I'm glad you said that," which will keep the discussion productive and moving forward. When you encourage people to be part of the solution, they'll feel more engaged and encouraged to work toward a successful resolution.

There may be times when you might have to halt a conflict resolution meeting to give everyone a chance to think about what's best for all involved before proceeding. If tempers flare or if people aren't willing to compromise, give everyone time to calm down by suspending the meeting for a short time. Say that you'd like to reschedule and that in the interim you'd like everyone to think objectively about what's best for all involved. If, after meeting again, it's still impossible to reach a solution, you may have to involve your boss or someone who can objectively mediate and make the final call in order to move forward.

Something to Think About

If you're responsible for facilitating a conflict resolution meeting, it may help to make a ground rule: no personal attacks, no button pushing, and no insulting, which shows everyone that you're focused on solving the problem.

Key Points

Practice the following when offering your best solution:

- After offering your best solution, ask if the other party or parties agree.
- If everyone agrees, then you're ready to move to the final step.
- If they don't agree, ask for other ideas.
- Allow everyone to propose a solution.
- Analyze the consequences of each proposal.
- Be respectful of everyone's opinion.
- Keep the focus on finding the best solution.
- Emphasize that this is not a blame game.
- Try to find common ground by looking for the things on which you can agree.

- Be prepared for give and take. Be the one to offer a compromise.
- If your role is to facilitate conflict resolution that doesn't directly involve you, maintain your objectivity.
- If the discussion stalls, postpone the meeting to give everyone a chance to calm down and look at the situation more objectively. In the event that you're not able to reach a compromise, involve someone with greater authority to mediate the meeting.

Offering Your Best Solution to the Problem

Dave continued. *"Let's talk about this and find the best solution.* (**compromise**) I'd like to propose that I'll do Diana's job and, if I have time, I'll help you by doing some of my work. What do you think about that? "

Tanya spoke up: "I understand it'll be difficult for you to do your job plus Diana's, but do you think you can guarantee that you'll do part of your workload every day?"

"If you could do that, I think it'd be a big help," Chad said. "Maybe you could do Diana's job in the morning and your work in the afternoon."

"Or maybe we could get together for a few minutes each morning and decide how to handle the work," Angela said. "I'm sure the three of us can do more to help out, and if you could pitch in when we need you that might solve the problem."

"Thanks for your input. I'll handle the job duties that Diana needs me to do, plus I'll guarantee you that I'll be able to pitch in with our workload. Chad, I'm concerned about agreeing to every afternoon, though, because I'll have a lot on my plate too. Angela, I like what you said about getting together every morning for a few minutes so we can talk about what each of us has scheduled for that day and decide how to share the work. Chad and Tanya, how do you feel about that?" (**compromise**)

Tanya smiled and nodded. Chad said: "That works for me."

Step 5: Agree on the Resolution

Step 4, which involves compromise, may be handled as swiftly as a short exchange of a few sentences between you and a coworker or among coworkers whose disagreement you are mediating. Or, it may be so involved it'll take more than one meeting to come to an agreement about the issue. Reaching an agreement depends on the problem, the people involved, and the willingness of everyone to cooperate. There are various ways to reach agreement, such as through consensus, by taking a vote, or having one person making the call. The optimum way is through consensus, whereby everyone has the opportunity to voice their opinion, everyone remains flexible, and everyone compromises. In some situations, however, someone may not compromise or agree to the solution. In those instances, ask if the person holding out will accept the final outcome and can live with the group consensus.

If consensus isn't achieved, you may have to resort to other measures, such as solving the problem the democratic way: everyone votes, majority rules. This may occur when a number of people are involved and it's difficult to get everyone to agree to a resolution. While this isn't as effective an approach as reaching consensus, if you do put the resolution to a vote, make sure you explain to those who aren't in agreement why the majority feels this is best. Often, when people understand the reasons behind a decision, they can buy into it.

You may also find yourself in situations in which you must make the decision. For example, the problem may be so out of control that the involved parties aren't able to communicate and aren't going to agree on anything. When you make the call, it's important to let everyone know you listened to their views and you made the best decision based on the input. It will help to begin by saying something like: "I've taken all of your opinions into consideration, but ultimately I had to make the decision and this is what it is…." Then explain why you made that decision and gain confirmation that everyone understands your reasoning.

In any conflict resolution situation, once you've arrived at an agreement, it's important to restate the resolution and make sure everyone buys into it. Give everyone the chance for additional input. The only way you'll put conflict to rest is by ensuring everyone is agreeable to the final decision. Approaching the situation with an open mind, fact finding to gain a better understanding, defining the problem from everyone's viewpoint, negotiating to reach an agreeable solution, and getting agreement on the resolution will help those involved move forward with confidence and strengthen work relationships.

Something to Think About

Most of your conflicts are likely to involve you and one other person rather than a group of coworkers. Thus, gaining agreement may involve more compromise on your part to reach a workable solution. But remember that in any conflict situation, it isn't about winning. It's about being open and flexible, respecting other people's points of view, and finding the solution that's best for all involved, even if it means backing down and not getting your way completely.

Key Points

Practice the following when agreeing on the resolution:

- Reach agreement through consensus, by taking a vote, or by one person making the call.
- Attempt to reach agreement through consensus, whereby everyone agrees on the final outcome.

- If you resort to deciding by majority rule, explain why the majority feels this is the best decision.

- If you have to make the final call, explain that you listened carefully to everyone's suggestions and made the best decision based on the information you had. Explain why you chose that decision.

- Once you've arrived at an agreement, restate the resolution and give everyone the chance for additional input to ensure that they buy into the final decision.

Gaining Agreement on the Outcome by Consensus, Vote, or One Person Making the Call

Dave was pleased with the resolution. *"Great. We're all in agreement. As soon as we're all here every morning, we'll get together and plan our work schedule. Then we'll jointly make a decision as to how we can help each other out. I appreciate that you're willing to work hard and I promise that I will, too."* (**resolution**)

Then he added: *"I'm so glad we talked this out. We're a strong team, and I feel that we're going to become even stronger now."* (**reconciliation**)

Resolving Conflict: The Right Way

Dave and his coworkers, Tanya, Chad, and Angela, are a cohesive, close-knit team. In the past, whenever a problem's come up, they've been able to work through it. But then Diana, Dave's boss, asked him to take over as team leader while she'll be out on a one-month maternity leave. Even though Dave is the newest member of the team, he felt proud that she chose him. He was confident that her decision was based on his demonstrating strong leadership skills, his knowledge about the job duties, and his role as the go-to person on the team.

As soon as his boss made the announcement, Dave immediately noticed a subtle change in his coworkers. During the meeting, Tanya looked down and didn't speak. Chad's facial expression became solemn and as he nodded his head slowly, he glanced at Angela, who raised her eyebrows and didn't look too happy either. After the meeting, Dave observed his coworkers huddled closely together. When he walked up to them, they stopped their conversation midsentence. Dave knew they were upset because he was chosen. He felt hurt that they weren't happy for him, but he knew that if he wanted the team to continue to operate efficiently and effectively, he'd need to talk with his team members and resolve the problem before it got out of hand.

First, he thought about how to proceed by evaluating each person's personality and how he or she was likely to respond. He kept his objectivity as he played out different scenarios. Then he planned how to open the discussion and how he'd work through the process to resolve the problem.

Dave told everyone he wanted to talk with them and called the team together in the conference room. He began: "When Diana made the announcement that I'd be taking over as team leader, *I felt that you were bothered by that decision, and I think we need to talk about this so we don't lose the closeness we've developed as a team*." (**"I" phrase**)

"It's important for us to be honest with each other," he continued, "so I'd like everyone to truthfully say how you feel about me being team leader."

No one spoke up, so Dave said: "Chad, will you start? Tell me how you felt when Diana made the announcement."

Chad shifted uncomfortably in his seat and responded: "Even though you're the newest member on the team, I understand why Diana chose you. What bothered me is that it isn't fair that the three of us are now going to have to do our work plus yours."

Dave nodded. *"I understand that."* (**understanding**) "Angela?"

"At first part of me felt it should have gone by seniority. Tanya's been here the longest. But that's not what bothered me the most. I agree with Chad. We've all got our plates full now. How are we supposed to take on more work?"

Dave turned to Tanya. "Do you agree with that?"

"Well, I don't agree that just because I've been here the longest I should have been chosen," Tanya said. "I think Diana made the right call when she picked you because you're the strongest member of our team. What bothered me is what Chad and Angela said. How are three people supposed to do the work of four?"

Dave took a moment to plan his response. Then he said: "Thanks for your input. I appreciate that you're supportive that I'll be team leader. I also appreciate your concern as to how the work's going to get done. Is that how all of you see it?"

He paid attention to their nonverbal signals as they each nodded in agreement. They seemed a little more relaxed now that Dave defined the problem.

"I certainly understand where you're coming from. **(understanding)** I assure you that I've already thought about that and it concerns me too. I feel strongly that we're going to resolve this issue so that we can all work together. Ultimately, when Diana comes back from maternity leave I want her to see that we're the same close-knit team we've always been."

Dave continued. *"Let's talk about this and find a solution we can all agree on.* **(compromise)** I'd like to propose that I'll do Diana's job and, if I have time I'll help you by doing some of my work. What do you think about that? "

Tanya spoke up: "I understand it'll be difficult for you to do your job plus Diana's, but do you think you can guarantee that you'll do part of your workload every day?"

"If you could do that, I think it'd be a big help," Chad said. "Maybe you could do Diana's job in the morning and your work in the afternoon."

"Or maybe we could get together for a few minutes each morning and decide how to handle the work," Angela said. "I'm sure the three of us can do more to help out, and if you could pitch in when we need you that might solve the problem."

"Thanks for your input. I'll handle the job duties that Diana needs me to do, plus I'll guarantee you that I'll be able to pitch in with our workload. Chad, I'm concerned about agreeing to every afternoon, though, because I'll have a lot on my plate too. Angela, I like what you said about getting together every morning for a few minutes so we can talk about what each of us has scheduled for that day and decide how to share the work. Chad and Tanya, how do you feel about that?"(**compromise**)

Tanya smiled and nodded. Chad said: "That works for me."

Dave was pleased with the resolution. *"Great. We're all in agreement. As soon as we're all here every morning, we'll get together and plan our work schedule. Then we'll jointly make a decision as to how we can help each other out. I appreciate that you're willing to work hard and I promise that I will, too."* (**resolution**)

Then he added: *"I'm so glad we talked this out. We're a strong team, and I feel that we're going to become even stronger now."* (**reconciliation**)

Why This Works

Because Dave took the time to plan his meeting, he was able to stay on track and work through the five steps. Even though his initial response was to feel hurt, he put his feelings aside, thought about the issue, and focused on how his coworkers likely viewed the situation. Then, he gathered the group together and addressed the issue by asking everyone to tell him what was bothering them. He listened carefully, paid attention to their nonverbal cues, and was able to define the problem and gain everyone's agreement. From there, he offered his best solution and then encouraged Chad, Angela, and Tanya to offer their solutions. Because this was a fairly simple issue to resolve, Dave quickly restated and ana-lyzed all the suggestions and then offered what he thought was the best solution based on what each member proposed. By remaining flexible and offering a compromise, Dave was able to gain agreement on the pro-posed resolution. Throughout his meeting, he relied on powerful phrases of understanding, compromise, resolution, and reconciliation. This team is now motivated to maintain its continuity and cohesiveness and, be-cause they talked through the problem, they're likely to continue their close-knit relationships with each other.

4

Powerful Phrases for Challenging Coworker Situations

Trying your best to get along with your coworkers is often difficult when they're bothersome, frustrating, or irritating. Some people can really get to you, whether it's a coworker who continually says or does things that upsets you or one whose aggravating habits drive you nuts. By empowering yourself with effective conflict resolution skills, you'll learn how to deal with other peoples' quirks and idiosyncrasies. This will help you get along with everyone at work. Then, when you incorporate powerful phrases into your conversations with coworkers and use effective nonverbal strategies to enhance your messages, you'll increase your ability to communicate well.

This chapter describes twenty coworker behaviors. You'll learn how to employ the five-step conflict resolution process to help you deal with these challenging situations. Sample dialogues are included for each of the annoying behaviors. As in the first three chapters, the powerful phrases are denoted in *italics* with the type powerful phrase noted in **(bold)**. For some of the behaviors, a "Something to Think About" helpful tip is included as well, demonstrating how to handle an unusual or difficult situation. Applying the five-step process to your interactions with coworkers will give you the confidence to successfully resolve any problem you encounter.

Basic Rules When Confronting a Coworker

When confronting a coworker about a problem, it's always best to focus on the situation rather than on the person. Your message will be better received if it shows that you viewed the situation from other perspectives, states how the offending behavior made you feel, and demonstrates a willingness to remain open. Keeping a relaxed and open demeanor, matching your facial expressions to the conversation, and speaking calmly and confidently can further increase your ability to make your feelings known and successfully handle any problem. This approach will enable you to resolve conflicts effectively and maintain strong, supportive relationships with your coworkers.

Before learning how to handle specific behaviors, here are some basic rules to remember when attempting to resolve a conflict:

- Always remain calm, no matter how the other person speaks to you.
- Always treat others with respect.
- Don't overreact.
- Take a wait-and-see approach whenever possible.
- Get a neutral person's perspective on the situation if you feel it'll help.
- Always speak in specifics and be prepared to share examples.
- Don't try to change people; focus only on changing the behavior.
- Avoid complaining about people to others.
- Not every situation needs to be addressed, even if you feel confident that you know how to effectively resolve conflict.

- Ignoring a situation may sometimes be your best option, particularly if it's the result of an annoying habit you can learn to ignore.

- Always give the person the chance to make things right; never go over someone's head without speaking to the involved person directly.

- If the situation can't be resolved after your resolution conversation, then and only then refer the matter to your boss.

- If the conversation heats up or you feel threatened, end the discussion and get someone else to mediate.

The following examples involve a conflict that arises between two employees, although the dialogue can be easily adapted for use in a group setting in which you're directly involved or responsible for mediating a conflict. But, when a group of coworkers has a problem with one other person, it's usually best to have one person confront the coworker. Otherwise, he or she may feel ganged up on and is likely to become defensive and noncommunicative.

How to Deal with a Backstabber

Amanda and Vicky had been working closely on a project for the past two weeks. During that time, Amanda got to know Vicky well and considered her more than a coworker; she considered Vicky her friend. Vicky had bragged to Amanda that she thought they were the two best employees and then said that the other members of their team were pretty much idiots. Although Amanda didn't consider herself a gossip, she found herself agreeing with Vicky when she'd talk about their coworkers. But then Amanda heard from another of their coworkers that Vicky had been badmouthing her, saying that her work on the project was substandard and that Amanda wasn't doing her share of the work. Amanda was flabbergasted. While she often agreed with Vicky that they were the two best members of their team, she didn't know why Vicky would stab her in the back, especially when she thought they worked well together.

If you work with someone who likes to talk about other people to you, chances are that person is going to talk about you to others, too. Some people like to put other people down, and they often do it to make themselves feel better, more important, or smarter. And, like Amanda, you may have enjoyed listening to the badmouthing. That is, until you heard that the person badmouthed you. You probably felt angry or hurt or indignant. What the person did was deceitful and underhanded. You wonder what else the person said about you that hadn't gotten back to you. The more you think about it, the more upset you become.

The best practice is not to talk negatively about anyone and don't enter into conversations with coworkers who talk about others. Stay above the fray. But even when you behave in this manner, at some time something someone said about you is going to get back to you. When it does, take action. Rather than retaliating and making a nasty comment about the backstabber, don't say anything until you've given yourself time to calm down. Then go directly to the backstabber. You need to stop this behavior, so discussing what you heard and giving the person a chance to respond gives you the edge in stopping future attacks by this person.

Amanda was hurt that Vicky would talk about her, especially when she thought they were friends. She wanted to immediately go to Vicky and tell her off, but didn't.

Step 1: Think First

Amanda took time to calm down. When she was able to think more clearly, she thought about how to handle the conversation she dreaded having with Vicky. She played out various scenarios and, when she approached Vicky, Amanda felt confident that she'd be able to handle the conversation well. She also knew that she'd have to present herself in an assertive manner. Otherwise, Vicky would have the upper hand in the conversation. Amanda made sure to maintain eye contact when she spoke.

Step 2: Gain a Better Understanding

"Vicky, someone told me that you said that my work on the project was substandard and that you're tired of having to do most of the work," Amanda said. "*I was stunned when I heard that, but mostly I was hurt that you'd talk about me like that.*" (**"I" phrase**)

Vicky shifted uneasily and looked down. Amanda wondered if Vicky was trying to gather her thoughts. "Who told you that?," Vicky asked.

Amanda was prepared for that question and wasn't going to deflect the conversation away from the badmouthing, so she replied: "It doesn't matter who told me. What matters is that you'd say something like that. Is that how you truly feel about working with me?"

"No. I don't remember saying that, but if I did I only said it as a joke," Vicky spoke adamantly.

Step 3: Define the Problem

"So what you're saying is that you don't remember but you may have made a joke about me?" Amanda asked.

"I might have. I really don't remember," Vicky responded.

"*Well, even making a joke about me bothers me because the person I heard it from didn't take it as a joke.* (**"I" phrase**) *I know that you're a good worker and you're very smart.* (**understanding**) But, so am I. And if we're going to work together, I don't appreciate having you joke about my work, especially when I know that we contribute equally to the project." Amanda was proud of the way she was handling the conversation by not letting Vicky off the hook or sidestep the issue. "Do you understand why hearing that bothered me so much?"

Vicky responded: "Yes, I do. If I said anything, I'm really sorry."

Step 4: Offer Your Best Solution

Amanda didn't back down. *"Thanks for apologizing. And, going forward, please come to me if you have any problems rather than talking or joking about me to other people."* (**compromise**)

Vicky seemed relieved. "I promise you that if I ever have a problem, I'll talk to you about it."

Step 5: Agree on the Resolution

"Good. (**resolution**) Amanda continued: *"I like working with you and don't want anything to come between our working relationship."* (**reconciliation**)

Why This Works

Had Amanda confronted Vicky when she was emotional, the conversation wouldn't have gone so smoothly. Amanda calmed down and then was able to think about the situation more objectively. She stated the facts of what she heard and allowed Vicky time to respond. She didn't take the bait when Vicky asked who told her that; doing so would have changed the focus of the dialogue. Amanda was assertive and remained calm throughout their conversation and was able to resolve the issue satisfactorily. But Amanda learned a valuable lesson about people who talk negatively about others. Going forward, she planned to take a different approach when Vicky talked about their coworkers by telling her she didn't want to hear those types of comments.

Something to Think About

Beware of agreeing with someone who's badmouthing another coworker. Word might get back to that person that you were the one who did the badmouthing, when you only agreed with what was said. Best practice: If someone says something about a coworker, stay neutral and don't offer your opinion unless it's to stand up for the person.

Applying the Approach

Apply the following principles when dealing with a backstabber:

- Don't fall into the trap of agreeing with someone who's badmouthing your coworkers.
- Don't confront the backstabber when you're upset or angry, which are normal emotions if you learn that someone badmouthed you.
- Do, however, plan to speak to the person.
- Give yourself time to calm down so that you can think about the conversation you need to have.
- Begin your conversation with the person by stating what you heard and how it affected you.
- Ask the person to explain.
- Make sure the backstabber understands what the problem is. The only compromise you should have to offer is that you expect him or her to come to you directly if he or she has a problem with you rather than talking about you behind your back.
- End the conversation with phrases of resolution and reconciliation.
- Keep this person at arm's length and watch what you say and how you act when together.

How to Deal with a Brownnoser

Lauren and her coworkers were becoming increasingly upset with their coworker, Mia, for her constant brownnosing. They tried applying peer pressure by making snide comments and rubbing their noses whenever Mia chummed up to their boss, Antonio, but nothing's worked. To make matters worse, Antonio loved the attention and began showing favoritism toward Mia. Last week, she started coming in 30 minutes late every day. When someone questioned her about it, she said, "I'm having trouble getting here earlier because I have to drop my baby off at daycare. I spoke to Antonio about it, and he's fine with me starting later. Besides, I'm going to make the time up at lunch so it's no big deal." But to her coworkers, it was a big deal. Mornings are the busiest time of day, and they could use the extra person to answer the early calls.

Brownnosers can be pretty irritating because they're in it for themselves. They flatter for favors. They suck up for personal gain. They grab the boss's attention through compliments and adulation. They fawn over those who can help them succeed. And they do it for selfish reasons: they want to gain an advantage, a promotion, or a special favor.

Applying peer pressure is often the most successful way to handle the office brownnoser. The group may make joking comments to the coworker. Someone may make the hand gesture of rubbing their nose in front of the team, whose members are likely to laugh at the brownnoser. Trying to embarrass a brownnoser may be effective, especially if he or she cares about the team. But, if the person is in it to seek a promotion or special favors from the boss, peer pressure may not work.

In that event, the best approach may be to ignore the brownnoser, focus on doing a good job and positioning yourself so that your boss sees your accomplishments. But if the boss is buying in to the brownnoser's flattery and begins showing favoritism, it's time to take action. In this situation, it's best to speak to your boss, because the brownnoser isn't going to stop the behavior as long as the boss is responding to it. Besides, if your boss is showing favoritism, it's your boss that you have the conflict with, not the brownnoser.

Lauren is the unofficial team leader, and she offered to speak to Antonio about this since it's affecting the team's productivity.

Step 1: Think First

Before going to Antonio, Lauren realized that she'd have to tread lightly. She didn't want to sound as though she was complaining or whining, so she decided to focus on the facts and approach him from the standpoint of how Mia's coming in late was affecting the entire team. Lauren met with Antonio in his office.

Step 2: Gain a Better Understanding

"I want to talk to you about something that's affecting our entire team," Lauren told him. "Mia's been coming in a half hour late every morning. She said it's okay with you, but it's really not okay with our team. *We have to handle the overload of calls that she should be helping answer, and it's starting to affect our workloads.*" (**"I" phrase**) Lauren maintained her composure, was assertive, and looked directly at Antonio as she spoke.

"Mia has a problem with dropping her baby off and getting here by 8:30," Antonio explained. "I agreed that she can start at nine and make up her time at lunch." Antonio looked directly at Lauren when he spoke. She could tell that he wasn't ready to back down.

"*I know full well it's an adjustment having a baby.* (**understanding**) I experienced that when I had my baby, but I dealt with it," Lauren responded. "In fact, I still have to drop my daughter off at daycare, but I'm able to make it to work on time."

Step 3: Define the Problem

Antonio didn't say anything, so Lauren continued. "I think I understand that from your point of view, you feel that it's all right for one member of our team to start later than the rest of us."

"Well, I hadn't thought about it that way," Antonio told her. "I was thinking it's more about my being flexible."

"Okay, sure," Lauren said. "So you're being accommodating because of Mia's baby."

Antonio nodded. Lauren felt that his nod was an agreement with her definition of the problem.

Step 4: Offer Your Best Solution

Lauren was prepared to offer a solution. *"I'd like to discuss this arrangement with you to see if we can find a solution that's agreeable to the entire team since none of the rest of us have flexible schedules,"* she continued. **(compromise)**

"I don't see what we need to talk about," Antonio countered. "She's going to make up the time."

"Here's where the team has a problem," replied Lauren. "When the office opens at 8:30 we're bombarded with calls. Early mornings are our busiest times. Without Mia here to help out, the rest of us are fielding additional calls and it's backing up our work for the day. By the time Mia comes in and actually starts taking calls, the rest of have four or five commitments already. *It's causing a hardship for us to get our work done. We appreciate that she has to get her baby to daycare, but I used to drop my baby off at the same daycare and made it on time. We really need her here when the office opens for business."* **("I" phrase, resolution)**

Antonio shifted uncomfortably in his chair. Lauren maintained eye contact and remained composed, sitting up straight and keeping a concerned facial expression.

"Well, I guess I hadn't thought how this was going to affect the team," Antonio said. "I see your point. I'll speak to Mia and tell her that I need her here at 8:30 when the rest of you start work. I didn't realize you had used the same daycare, so if you could do it she should have no problem getting here on time."

Step 5: Agree on the Resolution

"Thanks, Antonio, that sounds reasonable," Lauren said. *"We realize that every once in a while one of us is going to run into a problem, but as long as she can be here when the rest of us start, it'll help even out the workload for the day."* **(resolution)** *"I'm glad I talked to you about this. Our team has always worked well together, and I wouldn't want something like this to cause any problems.* **(reconciliation)**

Antonio responded, "Me too. I'm sorry that I handled this the way I did. I'll speak to Mia today."

Why This Works

Rather than becoming more disgruntled about Mia's brownnosing, the team decided to take action. There would have been no sense in saying anything to Mia, because Antonio bought into her brownnosing and began showing favoritism by allowing her to work a different schedule than was expected from the rest of the team members. There was no reason for Mia to change her tactics when they were working to her advantage. Lauren thought about how best to confront Antonio and decided to take a direct approach by explaining how his actions affected the team. Throughout her conversation, Lauren projected assertive body language by maintaining eye contact, sitting up straight, and keeping a concerned facial expression. She was able to communicate effectively that the rest of the team was handling a larger portion of the workload due to Mia's lateness. Antonio understood and agreed to speak to Mia.

While Mia may not be happy with the new arrangement, the team members agreed that after Antonio spoke to Mia, they would also speak to her and hopefully get her to understand that they all needed to work together as a team.

Applying the Approach

Apply the following principles when dealing with a brownnoser:

- Use peer pressure, as it is often effective when dealing with the team brownnoser.

- Try gentle chiding, joking, and rubbing one's nose, as these actions may help the brownnoser understand that the behavior is unacceptable to the team.

- Take action if the boss (or recipient of the brownnosing) starts buying in to it and begins showing favoritism.

- Recognize that the problem is now with the boss, who is granting special favors, so that's the person to speak to.

- Think before speaking, and remember to focus on how the boss's actions are affecting the rest of the team.

- Ask questions to gain a better understanding that will help you define the problem and also help get the boss to understand there is a problem.

- Be prepared to offer your best solution.

- Know that your efforts may fall on deaf ears. If the boss isn't willing to agree to your proposed solution, there's not a lot you can do.

- Well, actually there is. Focus on doing your best job and finding ways to showcase your accomplishments to your boss.

How to Deal with a Bully

Cindy dreaded going to work knowing that she'd have to put up with Diane's berating, demeaning, and humiliating behavior toward her. Cindy's job duties included creating invoices for Diane, who was responsible for completing and forwarding them to customers. Often, Diane would berate Cindy for not completing them on time, a claim that was unfounded. For whatever reason, Diane had singled Cindy out and made her the target of continuous disparagement. Cindy was a good worker, but she wasn't assertive or able to stick up for herself. She had tried ignoring Diane, hoping she'd stop. When she didn't, Cindy wished she could be as mean to Diane as Diane was to her, but it wasn't her nature to treat others in that manner, so she continued to put up with the bullying.

Unlike a criticizer who feels the need to harshly judge everyone, a bully singles out one person who becomes "prey." Bullies may hurl insults, display menacing behavior, show their dislike, act out disrespectfully, give dirty looks, or make fun of their target. They may also expect the victim to do their work and complain about how the victim works. In addition, they may overstep their boundaries in the victim's workspace by rummaging through papers or going through files without permission.

No one deserves to be bullied. And no one should suffer in silence. The most important rule to remember when dealing with a bully is that you need to put a stop to the behavior. When confronting a bully, stay calm and tell the person the behavior needs to end. Then, set boundaries for your working relationship. If the bullying continues, document each incident. If possible, ask a trusted coworker if he or she witnessed the behavior and would be willing to back you up. Discuss the bullying incidents with your boss or a human resources manager. Let the manager know that you've already confronted the bully, but the behavior hasn't stopped. Review your documentation with the manager and allow him or her to deal with the bully.

One of Cindy's coworkers had noticed the bullying and suggested to Cindy that she confront Diane. Even though it would be uncomfortable for Cindy to do that, she knew that's what she needed to do. She was tired of turning the other cheek only to be demeaned again. Because her feelings were slowly simmering toward anger, Cindy felt it best to approach Diane before she lost her cool and said something that could only make matters worse.

Step 1: Think First

Cindy talked to the coworker who said she should confront Diane. Together, they discussed the situation and ran through various conversations until Cindy felt comfortable saying what she wanted to say. She didn't feel a need to ask questions to better understand why Diane spoke to her as she did. There was no excuse for bullying, so she decided the best tactic would be to confront Diane the next time the bullying started, define the problem, and move to the solution step. She didn't have to wait long.

Step 2: Gain a Better Understanding

Not applicable, as explained in Step 1.

Step 3: Define the Problem

Diane soon walked past her desk and said: "I'm still waiting for today's invoices. What is your problem? Are you retarded or just slow?"

Cindy stood up, faced Diane, made eye contact, and replied: "I'm working on a project that has a higher priority. When I'm finished, I'll work on the invoices and get them to you."

Diane was nonplussed. "I need the invoices now so whatever you're working on, let it wait."

"No, Diane. I'm going to finish the project and then I'll get to the invoices. I'll have them to you this afternoon in plenty of time for you to complete them today." Cindy spoke as assertively as she could, maintaining eye contact, even though that was uncomfortable for her.

Diane glared at her. Even though Cindy felt her knees knocking, she said in her boldest voice: "Do you understand that I will get them to you in time for you to complete them?" Diane said nothing.

Cindy continued: *Diane, I don't know why you feel you have the right to treat me disrespectfully and, frankly, I don't care. I've put up with it long enough, and I need you to stop treating me this way."* (**"I" phrase**)

"I don't know what you're talking about." Diane glared at Cindy, expecting her to crack and back down.

"I'm sure you know exactly what I'm talking about," Cindy said. "I've taken your demeaning comments too long. I've put other work aside to get you the invoices when I know that you're demanding them just to give me a hard time. I do have other work, so going forward I'll get the invoices to you each day by early afternoon." Even though Diane never agreed she was causing a problem, Cindy felt confident that she had stated very clearly how Diane's behavior was affecting her.

Step 4: Offer Your Best Solution

Cindy felt her confidence grow as she offered her solution: *"Going forward, I expect you to treat me respectfully. If you don't or can't, then please don't say anything to me.* (**compromise**) *I don't deserve to be treated this way, and I'm not going to accept it anymore."* (**"I" phrase**)

Step 5: Agree on the Resolution

Diane gave her a dirty look, but walked away without saying a word. Cindy felt empowered that she had finally spoken up and, even though Diane hadn't agreed, Cindy felt that Diane understood her resolution loud and clear. As for offering a phrase of reconciliation, Cindy wanted to wait and see if Diane's behavior changed for the better. If it did, she'd offer one when one was warranted.

Why This Works

Successfully confronting a bully requires that you maintain a calm and assertive demeanor, speaking confidently and candidly. Because she had practiced with a coworker, Cindy was able to say what she wanted to say to Diane. She didn't beat around the bush or belabor the point, but spoke straightforwardly. She explained the problem, stated that she was no longer willing to be bullied, told Diane the behavior needed to stop, and let her know when she could expect the invoices. Before the confrontation, Cindy had also begun documenting each incident. She wasn't sure the bullying would stop, so she was prepared to take the next step and go to her manager with the documentation if necessary.

Applying the Approach

Apply the following principles when dealing with a bully:

- Try ignoring the behavior in hope that the bully will grow tired of your failure to respond and stop.

- If the behavior continues, remind yourself that you don't deserve to be treated this way.

- If your place of business has formal procedures about bullying, then you may decide to go directly to your boss or human resources without confronting the person.

- If you decide to confront the bully, there's no need to work through the phases of fact finding and defining the behavior.

- Practice your conversation so that you're able to stay calm and in control when you speak to the bully.

- Remember that the most empowering words you need to say are: "The behavior needs to stop." If you feel the need or if the bully denies the behavior, give examples.

- Understand that you may not get the bully to back down and agree that the behavior was out of line.

- Be prepared to offer your resolution by stating specifically how you expect to be treated.

- If the bullying continues, document each incident. Your documentation should speak for itself so include date and time, what the person said or did, and if there were any witnesses to the conversation.

- Then, speak to your boss or a human resources manager.

How to Deal with a Credit Taker

Earlier in the day, the vice president of the company visited the field office. Kayla and her coworkers were busy doing their jobs while Julie, the most outgoing team member, was promoting herself to the VP. Kayla and her coworkers looked at each other in astonishment as they listened to Julie tell the VP about the directory she created because their entire team had contributed to the project. And, it wasn't even Julie's idea. Kayla wanted to step up, join the conversation, grab some of the spotlight back, and give credit where credit was due but she, like her coworkers, kept quiet.

Dealing with a credit taker may be one of the most aggravating behaviors you'll come across at work. You know the type. When your boss or a member of upper management visits your office, the credit taker shines the spotlight directly on himself or herself for work on which you helped or for which you were solely responsible. You watch dumbfounded, so shocked that your coworker would do this that you're speechless. Credit takers may take many shapes, including a coworker who asks for your help but doesn't acknowledge your contributions, a team member who takes 100 percent credit for completing a project your team worked on, or the person with the gift of glib talk who knows how to promote himself or herself to the omission of everyone else.

We've all worked with credit takers. We've all been frustrated by them. And we've all been caught off guard and allowed the person to steal the spotlight from us. The most effective way to handle a credit taker is to be prepared and speak up during the credit taking process.

Kayla didn't think quickly enough to speak up and give the team credit for the project. What Julie did was not fair, as she undermined the entire team. The group was so upset that the members talked about what happened when Julie went on break. Rather than having the entire team confront Julie, Kayla offered to speak to her one on one.

Step 1: Think First

Before Kayla approached Julie, she thought about the situation. She found it difficult to understand Julie's perspective because she would never behave that way. She decided to let Julie know how everyone felt, ask her to explain, and go from there. But she was also determined to get Julie's agreement that she wouldn't do this again.

Step 2: Gain a Better Understanding

After taking a deep breath, Kayla approached Julie: "I want to talk to you about what happened when Mr. Sanders was in the office today. Do you have a minute now?"

Julie nodded, and Kayla said, "Let's go into the conference room so we can talk quietly."

After closing the door, Kayla continued: "*When I heard you take all the credit for the directory our team created, I was really shocked and so was the rest of our team. We all felt betrayed that you'd do that.*" (**"I" phrase**) She spoke assertively, remained calm, and kept her facial expression neutral. "Rather than everyone talking to you about this, I volunteered to speak for the team."

"I didn't realize I did that," Julie countered casually. "Sorry."

"You mentioned that you didn't realize you did that, and *I can un-*

derstand how that could happen (**understanding**), but I'm wondering why you would take sole credit for a team project," Kayla said.

"It wasn't a big deal," Julie replied. "I'm sure Mr. Sanders knew that it was a group effort. I just happened to be the one available to tell him about it."

Step 3: Define the Problem

"Okay," Kayla said. "So what you're saying is that you didn't realize you took all the credit and that you were the one available so you became the team spokesperson."

Julie shrugged her shoulders and nodded. She looked uncomfortable.

Kayla didn't let her off the hook. "Do you agree with that?"

Julie said: "Yeah, I guess so. I certainly wouldn't do anything to undermine the team. I just happened to be available when Mr. Sanders stopped by."

Step 4: Offer Your Best Solution

"Look Julie, *we need to find a solution so this doesn't happen again,*" Kayla continued. (**compromise**) "*Especially since everyone on our team felt angry and betrayed that you spoke only of your accomplishments rather than the group's.*" (**"I" phrase**)

"I'm sorry," Julie said. "What more can I say?"

"*Going forward, we'd like your assurance that if you happen to be the one speaking for the team, you'll give credit to the entire group.*" responded Kayla. "*Speak in terms of 'we' rather than 'I'.* (**compromise**) Had you done that this time we wouldn't have been upset. Will you agree to that?"

Step 5: Agree on the Resolution

Julie nodded. "Now I can see how what I did bothered everyone. Going forward, I'll make sure that I speak more carefully and include all of us."

"That sounds great," Kayla said. *"I'm glad we talked this out, and I'm also glad that you understand how what you did made us feel.* (**resolution**) *We've always been a strong team and now that we talked this out we can only become stronger."* (**reconciliation**)

"I'm going to apologize to everyone right now," Julie promised.

Why This Works

Because Kayla volunteered to speak to Julie, it didn't appear as though the entire team was pouncing on her. Kayla spoke assertively and remained calm. She was prepared for Julie's answer that she didn't do it on purpose and then asked Julie if she realized how that made the team feel. Kayla didn't back down, but offered the suggestion that in the future, Julie speak in terms of the entire team rather than only of herself. When Julie agreed, Kayla offered phrases of resolution and reconciliation that ended their meeting on a positive note. By offering to apologize to the team, Julie isn't likely to take credit for team accomplishments in the future.

Something to Think About

Credit takers are in it for themselves and don't really care about others. Consider that any time you approach a credit taker your coworker may become dismissive, as Julie was, or defensive. Be ready for these likely scenarios and you'll be prepared to continue your discussion in an assertive, confident manner.

Applying the Approach

Apply the following principles when dealing with a credit taker:

- Be on your guard. Circumvent your coworker by speaking up and taking or giving credit where credit is due.

- Look for opportunities to showcase your own accomplishments. Often, credit takers are the more gregarious members of the group and find it easy to shine the spotlight on themselves.

- Practice tooting your own horn by thinking through some scenarios and how you might speak positively about yourself. Practicing will help you learn how to promote your accomplishments in a modest manner, so that it doesn't sound as though you're bragging.

- If the credit taker gets one (or more) past you, it may be time to address the issue by speaking to the person. Explain how it made you feel and follow the five-step process to negotiate a successful conclusion. And, if it's a group situation, the better approach is to have one person speak for the group.

- If, after speaking to the credit taker, the behavior doesn't stop, stay on your guard. Be prepared to offer your input when the credit t starts again.

- Bottom line, don't be a wallflower. Be assertive and speak up for yourself because if you don't, upper management may never realize your contributions.

How to Deal with a Criticizer

The first time Mark criticized Vince, a new employee, Vince didn't reply. He figured that Mark was either having a bad day or didn't know that Vince had only been partially trained. The second time Mark criticized him, Vince apologized and commented that he'd be glad when he received the rest of his training. This morning Mark again lashed out at Vince in front of some of their team members about work he had done, and then loudly asked him: "Why did you do that?" Vince felt the question was derogatory and out of line; he'd had enough of Mark's criticizing. Vince won-

dered: Was Mark going to continually take potshots and belittle him just because he wasn't as experienced?

Some people are born criticizers. While some people talk about others behind their backs, criticizers have no problem taking the talk directly to the person. They take potshots, rely on cheap shots, and use sarcasm when speaking. If they don't speak directly to the person, they make aside comments loud enough for the person to hear. As in Vince's case, a criticizer may feel more comfortable picking on new employees because they're an easy target. In other cases, it doesn't matter how new or experienced an employee is. A criticizer may still feel the need to continually berate, challenge, or disparage a coworker. Some people criticize others because they feel the need to "help," but don't have the filter to screen how best to offer help. Others may criticize to make themselves feel superior. And, some people criticize because they feel it's their "job" to point out other people's insecurities and shortcomings.

Whatever the reason for a person's criticizing, it can be very tiring, whether you're a new employee who hasn't yet found your comfort level at work or an experienced employee who knows what you're doing. The first time someone criticizes you, the best response may be no response. Or, if you feel the need to reply, you might say: "Thank you for your opinion." This will likely leave the person speechless and end the conversation. Then you can decide whether the criticism is valid. If it is, you need to decide how to act on it. In the case of a constant criticizer like Mark, you can either continue to ignore the person, continue to thank the person for his or her opinion, or enter into a conflict resolution conversation.

Vince had grown tired of Mark's daily criticisms. When Mark called him out in front of their coworkers, he felt it was time to talk to Mark and let him know that he didn't appreciate the daily criticisms, especially since he was new and still getting his bearings.

Step 1: Think First

Vince also didn't want to alienate Mark, whom he knew to be an experienced colleague who could be a big help to him. Vince decided to let Mark know how the constant criticizing made him feel, yet also convey to Mark that he respected his knowledge. Vince thought about how to tell Mark how he'd like to be treated going forward. When he felt comfortable working through the conversation in his head, he spoke to Mark.

Step 2: Gain a Better Understanding

"Mark, if you have a few minutes I'd like to talk to you about something."

"Sure, what's up?"

"Since I started working here, you've criticized my work repeatedly. *This morning when you called me out in front of other coworkers, that was out of line. It really bothered me that you'd do that, considering I've only been on the job a few weeks.*" (**"I" phrase**) Vince did his best to maintain good posture, make eye contact, and keep a concerned facial expression.

"Hey, I was only joshing with you," Mark responded.

"It wasn't funny to me." Vince felt that Mark said that to appease him. Vince wasn't about to back down.

Mark said: "Lighten up a little. You've got to know I was only joking."

Step 3: Define the Problem

Vince replied: *"If you meant that as a joke, I now have a better understanding of where you were coming from.* (**understanding**) And, my understanding is that your idea of joking is to call someone out in front of other people."

Mark shrugged and laughed uneasily.

Step 4: Offer Your Best Solution

Vince was glad that he had rehearsed what he wanted to say because he was very comfortable when he continued. *"Being a new employee and not knowing as much as the rest of you already puts me in an uncomfortable position. But Mark, no one has a right to criticize me like you did, joking or not. I'd like us to agree on how we communicate with each other going forward."* (**compromise**)

"Okay, I get it. I'm sorry if I took a joke too far. I won't do it again," Mark said.

"I respect that you're very knowledgeable, and I'd like to know that I can come to you when I need help. *Can we agree that in the future I can count on you to speak to me in a more constructive manner?"* Vince spoke confidently, pleased that he handled the conversation in an assertive manner. (**compromise**)

Step 5: Agree on the Resolution

"Of course. Again, I'm sorry I took the joking too far."

"I'm glad we talked this out. (**resolution**) *And I'm glad I can count on your help too."* (**reconciliation**)

Why This Works

If the criticisms were one time or random, Vince may have chosen to ignore the comments. But when Mark criticized him in front of their coworkers, Vince felt that the personal attacks weren't going to stop. He assumed the reason for the disparaging comments was that he was the new kid on the block, but Mark still had no right to treat him that way. Vince thought about what he wanted to say so he was prepared when Mark brushed off the comments as jokes. Vince stated how the criticisms made him feel, was able to get Mark to understand the problem, and assertively said that in the future he'd like to be treated more respectfully. He also threw Mark an olive branch by complimenting him on his job knowledge. By doing this, he let Mark know that he valued him as a coworker and wanted to count on him for assistance.

Applying the Approach

Apply the following principles when dealing with a criticizer:

- The first time someone criticizes you, choose whether you want to ignore the remark or act on it.

- If you choose to respond, try saying: "Thank you for your opinion." This is apt to end the conversation.

- Whenever someone criticizes you, view the criticism a growth opportunity. Analyze the criticism. If it's valid, decide what you can do to improve.

- If you need additional training to correct the problem, ask for it.

- If the criticisms continue and have no validity, you can continue ignoring the criticizer, continue thanking the person for his or her opinion, or decide to confront the person.

- Before entering into a conflict resolution discussion, think through the likely conversation.

- You may catch the criticizer off guard, and the person may respond as Mark did by brushing off the criticisms as jokes. Don't let the person off the hook or the behavior is apt to continue.

- Make sure the person understands why the criticisms create a problem for you.

- State specifically how you expect to be treated.

- Agree on a resolution and offer a phrase of reconciliation.

How to Deal with an Ethics Violator

Melanie was completing an order when she overheard her coworker, Todd, say to his customer: "If you buy this today I'll waive the installation fee." Melanie's mouth dropped open because it wasn't company policy to offer free installation as a customer incentive. She waited for Todd to complete his call and then said: "Hey, Todd. I overheard you offer free installation to your customer. What's up with that?" Todd winked at her and said: "Hey, if it'll close the deal, why not? She was ready to buy anyway. I just helped her speed up her decision. I'm going to note the account that this customer was irate to cover my butt." Melanie didn't say anything else but the more she thought about their conversation the more she realized that Todd crossed the ethical boundary. And, because he was noting the account, she felt certain that he also knew it was wrong.

Some people feel that rules are made for everyone else. Some don't really understand the seriousness of ethics. And, some just don't seem to know there's a fine line between right and wrong. If you work with someone who crosses the ethical line, then it's your responsibility to do something. Whether it's a coworker who, like Todd, offers a special deal to make a sale or bends the rules to fit the situation, crossing the ethical line is a serious violation of company policy. While you're not the police, judge, or jury, when you become aware that someone is doing something ethically wrong, you become responsible for addressing the issue.

Unless it's a serious violation, you should first deal with an ethics violator by speaking to the person directly. Perhaps he isn't aware that what he's doing is ethically wrong. Or, perhaps she's under the misunderstanding that her conduct falls within company guidelines. Take the person aside, and ask questions to find out the reason for the ethics violation. Then explain the impact on other customers and coworkers. Follow the steps below to resolve the issue. If, after speaking to your coworker, the behavior doesn't stop, refer the problem to your boss to handle. Be sure to document your conversation to avoid any future ramifications that may implicate you.

Melanie didn't regret delving more deeply into the matter when she first confronted Todd because it gave her time to think about the best way to handle the situation. She prepared herself to bring it up again later that afternoon.

Step 1: Think First

Melanie wanted to handle the situation in a way that would help her better understand why Todd did what he did, as well as to make him understand the need to take responsibility for violating company policy. She ran through the conversation in her mind, which gave her confidence when she addressed the issue.

Step 2: Gain a Better Understanding

Melanie said: *"Todd, I've thought about our conversation this morning, and it's been bothering me.* **("I" phrase)** *I realize that you waived the installation fee to close the deal,* **(understanding)** *but what bothers me is that it's not what the rest of us are offering, and it's going to inflate your sales results.* **("I" phrase)** She continued: "I'm wondering why you'd do that."

Todd answered: "We're under a lot of pressure to produce. I don't see anything wrong with bending the rules if it means getting the sale. Besides, in the long run, I don't understand why it isn't company policy. After all, we'll more than make up for the installation fee if we can get the customer to buy from us rather than go to our competition."

Step 3: Define the Problem

Melanie looked directly at Todd when she continued. "I see. So you feel that there's nothing wrong with bending the rules, even though the rest of us aren't doing that."

Todd sat silently, his brows furrowed. He shrugged his shoulders and replied: "I only did it this one time."

"But again, you're okay with doing something like that even if it's only one time?" Melanie asked.

Todd looked down. "I see where you're coming from."

Step 4: Offer Your Best Solution

Melanie then said: *"Even one time doesn't make it right. What you did isn't fair to other customers who aren't offered the same deal. And it isn't fair to the rest of us because we're following company policy.* **("I" phrase)** *We need to resolve this and, from my viewpoint, the only solution is that this can't happen again."* **(compromise)**

Melanie stopped before saying that if it didn't stop she would go to their boss. She wanted to give Todd a chance to respond.

Step 5: Agree on the Resolution

Todd said: "I never thought about it that way. You're right. I won't do it again."

Melanie smiled and said: *"Great. I'm glad we talked this out, and I'm glad you understand how damaging doing something like this can be.* **(resolution)** *I didn't want to take it to our boss before I had a chance to speak with you. We work closely together, and I don't want to jeopardize our working relationship."* **(reconciliation)**

"I appreciate that. Thanks, Mel."

"You're welcome. But one more thing, Todd. I think you need to come clean, tell our boss why you did it, and assure her that you won't do it again,"

"Sure. You're right. I'll go talk to her now."

Melanie was pleased that Todd agreed to stop and to talk to their boss about what happened.

Why This Works

Once Melanie overheard Todd cross the ethical boundary, she became responsible for handling the issue. Rather than going over his head to their boss, she decided to speak directly to Todd. She gave him a chance to explain, defined the problem, and gained his agreement that what he did was wrong. Then she offered a strong compromise solution. Even though he did seem to understand and agreed to her solution, Melanie felt it was necessary to take the extra step and tell him he needed to talk to their boss.

Applying the Approach

Apply the following principles when dealing with an ethics violator:

- If you know about an ethical violation and ignore the situation, it may have negative repercussions for you.

- As soon as you become aware of an ethics violation, you become responsible for addressing or referring the issue.

- If you feel comfortable addressing the issue with your coworker, especially if the coworker may not know the conduct was improper, do so right away. Don't take a wait-and-see approach. But, first work through your conversation in your mind. This help you gain the confidence needed to speak assertively.

- Always give the other person the chance to explain, as this will help you better understand.

- Define the problem as it affects the company, other employees, and customers.

- The only compromise you will offer (and it isn't really a compromise, but rather a strong statement), is that the violation must never happen again.

- After you gain agreement from your coworker, clearly state that the offender needs to talk to your boss about it. Taking this step places the responsibility on the violator and also on the boss. If the violation is very serious or it's a dicey situation in which you don't feel comfortable speaking to your coworker, then address the issue with your boss.
- Make sure you have documentation to back up your accusation.

How to Deal with an Excessive Emailer

Leah opened her email inbox and muttered under her breath when she saw that 24 of the emails were sent by Richard that morning. He simply didn't seem to understand email etiquette. He felt the need to share every email he received, often using the "reply all" function, even when it wasn't necessary for everyone to read his reply. He often shared jokes and cc'd everyone. The email overload was causing Leah grief. Her day was busy enough without wading through the excess of emails Richard felt the need to send.

Email etiquette means to be mindful when sending and forwarding emails, yet many people don't understand the basic rules. They feel the need to bombard their coworkers with too many emails. They send out blanket emails rather than asking themselves: do the intended recipients really need to read this? They may muddle up their subject line to the point of confusion so the recipient has to open the email to see if the content is valid. They may ramble and write too much text when a few words would be appropriate. They use "reply all" when a "reply" sent to specific people is a better approach. And they forward personal jokes, chain mail, and other needless drivel to their coworkers who are already laden with too much email. If you work with an excessive emailer, then you were most likely nodding your head when you read the descriptions of the abusers.

If you're on the receiving end of a coworker who is an excessive emailer, you have a choice. You can delete the emails without reading them or add a spam filter, which may come back to bite you sometime if the person sends a valid email that you haven't seen. You can open each email and quickly scan the content, but this take valuable time. Or, you can speak to your coworker and explain email etiquette.

Leah had gotten into the habit of deleting all of Richard's emails as unnecessary reading. Then, one day last week, she missed an essential email that he had sent. Because she hadn't opened it, she came to a meeting unprepared to discuss an important topic. She felt she had made herself look weak, so since then she has opened every email and scanned the content. But that was taking too much time and she was getting tired of all the jokes and forwarded nonsense that Richard sent.

Step 1: Think First

Leah pondered the best way to handle the situation. She decided to address the problem head on, explain to Richard why this was causing a problem for her, and then tell Richard very specifically what types of emails she wanted to receive.

Step 2: Gain a Better Understanding

"Richard, do you have a minute? I'd like to talk to you about something," Leah approached Richard toward the end of their workday.

"Yeah, but only if it's quick. I have a lot of emails I have to get through," he replied.

"That's exactly what I want to speak to you about. *I've only got so many hours to get all my work done and the number of emails you're forwarding is consuming too much of my time. I'm having a problem finishing my work and that's starting to stress me out.*" (**"I" phrase**)

"Tell me about it! I have to read each of those emails before I send them on," Richard laughed. He didn't appear to take Leah seriously.

Step 3: Define the Problem

"Richard, I'm serious about this," Leah told him. "I do have a problem with receiving so many emails. I'll admit I started deleting most of your emails, but last week when I hadn't read the one that directly affected the discussion during our meeting, I realized that wasn't the right thing to do. On the other hand, I just don't have that kind of time to wade through so many emails, and if you're running behind at the end of the day because you have to read your emails, then it sounds as if you don't, either."

"I've never thought about it that way but yeah, I guess I have to agree with you," Richard said. "I get a lot too, maybe too many. But I do enjoy reading the jokes and I thought you did, too."

Step 4: Offer Your Best Solution

"I appreciate that and I see where you're coming from. **(understanding)***. But here's how I see it. While I enjoy good jokes, I don't enjoy them when they fill up my inbox. Let's see where we can come together on this."* **(compromise)** Leah hoped he understood and she continued in a confident tone. *"Going forward, I'd only like to receive business-related emails that I really need to read."* **(compromise)**

"Well, okay. But how am I to know what you need to see and what you don't?" Richard asked.

Leah replied: *"Let's just leave it as anything business related, with a few exceptions. If you're replying to an email, you probably don't need to reply to everyone. When you're writing an email that I do need to read, it would help if you keep the text short and to the point. And, as I said, as much as I enjoy a good joke, I don't enjoy them when they fill up my inbox, so no jokes, please."* **(compromise)**

Step 5: Agree on the Resolution

Leah continued: *"Can we please agree to that?"* **(resolution)**

"Sure. I guess I've been guilty of taking the easy way out and forwarding stuff before taking the time to think about it. I promise I won't send you any more jokes, and I'll filter all emails before sending them to you," Richard agreed.

"Thank you. I'm glad we talked about this. It may save you some time, too." Leah responded. (**reconciliation**) "And if it's a really good joke, share it with me at break, okay?"

Richard laughed. "You got it."

Why This Works

Leah had gotten into the habit of deleting all of Richard's emails but when she came to a meeting unprepared, she realized that wasn't the right approach. As a result, she began scanning every email to see if the content was valid. But that, too, wasn't the right approach because it was again taking up too much of her time. Because Leah stated specifically why this had become a problem, she was able to get Richard to agree with her. She was prepared to tell him what types of emails she wanted to receive, and they were able to reach a resolution. Leah ended the conversation on a positive note and made Richard feel valued when she asked him to share the good jokes when they went to break.

Applying the Approach

Apply the following principles when dealing with an excessive emailer:

- In a work situation, don't decide to delete all emails from the offender. Some may be important.
- If you don't have time to scan every email from an email offender, talk to the person.
- Tell the person that you don't have the time to read unimportant emails that don't pertain to work. Explain why it's a problem for you. Get the person's buy-in that they understand.

- Offer a compromise by stating specifically the types of emails you want to receive.

- If you don't feel it's necessary to be cc'd on replies, say so.

- Always rule on the side of caution. You want to make sure you see the emails that may be pertinent, so make sure the person understands what you do need to see before ending your conversation and offering a phrase of reconciliation.

How to Deal with a Gossipmonger

Nick works in an office that employs over 100 employees. He tries to mind his own business and stay away from the grapevine chatter. He prides himself on being congenial to all of his coworkers, but of all the employees in the office, he wishes Brian, didn't occupy the cubicle next to his. Nick has grown tired of listening to Brian gossip about the goings on in—and out of—the office. He's tried to ignore him and has even pretended to be on calls whenever Brian pokes his head in his cubicle, but Brian somehow manages to corner him to share the latest news. Nick's aggravation turned to anger when Brian couldn't wait to say that someone told him that one of their coworkers was in big trouble and might get suspended for messing up an important report. Nick doesn't want to listen to gossip, and he really doesn't want to hear negative hearsay about a coworker he likes and respects. Nick walked away without defending the coworker but was sorry he didn't speak up because he knew that it wouldn't be long before Brian shared the next tidbit.

Like Brian, some people just like to gossip. They can't wait to share the latest news, even when it's hearsay and may not be accurate. They want to be part of the grapevine, the dispensers of information, the bearers of good—and bad—facts, rumors, and innuendos. Even if you like to hear gossip or inadvertently get caught up in the office grapevine, in the long run it's best to not involve yourself in this useless blather. It's also best not to repeat gossip you've heard. Someone might repeat something you said about another person that gets back to that person and accuse you of instigating nasty rumors. Or, another person can take something that you said out of context, and you'll find yourself needing to defend yourself. If any of these events occur, your coworkers and boss will lose trust in you.

So how do you avoid gossip? Just ignore the banter. Don't comment or make facial gestures that communicate your feelings. Remain calm, keep a passive facial expression, and if someone asks your opinion or goads you into agreeing, you can say: "I don't know enough about the situation to comment." By remaining neutral, you'll let others know that you're not into gossip. If someone continuously gossips to you, as in Nick's case, it's probably best to ignore the person. The gossipmonger is looking for a response. So don't provide one. Don't raise your eyebrows or look shocked. By remaining unresponsive, the gossipmonger may get the hint and take the gossip elsewhere.

Nick knew that unless he spoke up, Brian wasn't going to stop gossiping. He decided to speak to Brian and tell him he didn't want to hear any more bad news about their coworkers and other office chatter.

Step 1: Think First

Nick figured that nothing he could say would change Brian's behavior. His goal in speaking up was twofold: he wanted to directly address the rumor involving the coworker whom Brian said was in hot water, and he wanted to make sure Brian understood that going forward he didn't want to listen to any gossip. Nick played out the conversation in his mind, focusing on how it affected him and how the conversation might affect Brian.

Step 2: Gain a Better Understanding

When Brian poked his head in Nick's cubicle later that day to provide an update on the coworker, Nick spoke up. "Brian, come in and sit down. I'd like to talk to you about something."

Brian looked excited as he sat down, ready to spill all the details. "You wouldn't believe what...."

Nick interrupted him and said, "Look, Brian, I didn't ask you in to tell me all the dirty details. *I like John a lot, and it bothered me when you told me he was in trouble.* **("I" phrase)** In fact, I really don't like hearing any office gossip. *I'm here to do my job. When you told me about him it bothered me and threw me off when I tried to refocus on my work.*" **("I" phrase)**

"I'm only repeating what I heard about John. It's not like I'm making this stuff up. Just want to keep you up to speed, Bro."

Step 3: Define the Problem

Nick nodded, kept a neutral facial expression, and continued. "So what you're saying is that you're repeating things you hear to keep me informed, whether or not the information has been verified. And you're telling me whether or not I'm in the middle of completing an important project."

"Well, when you put it like that, no I don't verify everything. I figure if someone tells me something it's true. And I didn't realize that I threw you off."

Nick added: "So you do you understand my position. You understand how hearing unwanted gossip can interfere with me getting back into the work mode?"

"Well, I hadn't thought about that, but I guess so," Brian said.

Step 4: Offer Your Best Solution

Nick leaned forward and said: *"I can appreciate that you want to keep me informed about what's going on.* **(understanding)** *But Brian, as I said, I really don't want to know everyone else's business. I'd prefer if you didn't* *tell me anything about anyone in the office. I'd rather talk about other things or else just sit here and do my job."* (**compromise**)

"Well, if you don't want to hear any office news and you're so busy working maybe I just shouldn't talk to you at all," Brian countered.

Nick had prepared himself for that type of defensive response. "Brian, I don't want you to take this the wrong way. *I like you. I enjoy working with you. I like talking to you. But I just don't like hearing rumors and gossip about anyone. As long as we can keep our conversations on other topics, I'd appreciate that. It will help keep my head clear for work, too."* (**compromise**)

Step 5: Agree on the Resolution

"Well, sure," Brian said. "I can live with that."

Nick smiled and said: *"Great.* (**resolution**) *I'll enjoy our conversations a lot more when they don't involve our coworkers."* (**reconciliation**)

"I understand."

Why This Works

Nick's purpose for having the conversation wasn't to change Brian's behavior. It was merely to change the topic of their conversations to avoid gossip. He clearly stated how hearing the rumor about the coworker had made him feel. He also explained that he didn't want to listen to gossip of any kind because it affected his ability to complete his work. When Brian became defensive, Nick was prepared. So, he offered an assurance and was able to turn the conversation around. Nick ended their interaction by reiterating that he'll enjoy their conversations more when they don't involve gossip. When Brian reaffirmed that he understood the dialogue ended on a positive note.

Applying the Approach

Apply the following principles when dealing with a gossipmonger:

- Try ignoring the gossip. Remain neutral and don't offer your opinion. Keep a passive facial expression and don't use gestures that indicate agreement or surprise.
- If someone asks for your opinion, tell them you'd rather not comment.
- If the gossipmonger is starting to get to you and is affecting your work, you need to speak up.
- Tell the person that you don't care to listen to any gossip and explain how it affects your work.
- Get the person to agree with how you defined the problem.
- Then offer a compromise.
- Gain agreement that the person will leave you out of the loop.
- If you find that listening to grapevine news and other gossip continues to be bothersome when you're with a group, it may be time to avoid the group.
- Consider this: If you hang with people who gossip, others are going to assume you're just like them.

How to Deal with a Know-It-All

Grace has been doing her job for three years. She's an experienced employee and rarely has to ask for help. Her boss has assigned her additional projects, and she's felt proud to have completed them successfully. She's also filled in for the boss when he's been on vacation. Grace works well with her team members and feels they respect her… all except Kyle, the team know-it-all. She's about had it up to her eyeballs with Kyle, whose superior atti-

tude and desire to treat others as though they don't know how to do their jobs has gotten to her. She's talked to a couple of her coworkers about it, and they feel the same.

Know-it-alls think they know everything. They feel superior, are dismissive of others' opinions, are unwilling to listen to others, and love to tell others how to do their job. Know-it-alls like to hear themselves talk. This behavior may become so ingrained that it becomes part of the know-it-all's personality. The bottom line is that they don't know any other way to act. They come off as self-centered and pompous and easily irk you, especially if you know how to do your job well. You bite your tongue when he starts telling you what you already know. You bristle when she talks down to you. But there's an effective way to deal with the know-it-all, to gently put them in their place without sounding like a know-it-all yourself.

The key to dealing with these types is to use tact and assertiveness. When the know-it-all tells you how to do your job, speak up, say thank you, and then add that if you need help you'll be sure to ask. This may put an end to the behavior. If it doesn't, take the person aside and have a heart to heart. Explain how his actions make you feel. Allow him to save face by acknowledging that you think he's smart. But be prepared, because the person may not to back down and take responsibility.

In addition, understand that you're not going to completely change this person's behavior toward others. Your goal is to stop the behavior that's directed at you. If you're able to do that, then you'll be able to move forward and work with your coworker on a level playing field.

Grace has tactfully mentioned to Kyle that if she needs help she'll ask him, but he's continued to treat her as though she doesn't know what she's doing. Earlier today, during a meeting, Kyle alluded to the fact that he helped Grace complete a project when he hadn't. She fumed and decided it was time to confront him directly.

Step 1: Think First

Before Grace approached Kyle, she took time to calm down and diffuse her anger. She thought about what she was going to say and also how he'd respond. Thinking about the situation increased her confidence when she spoke to him.

Step 2: Gain a Better Understanding

When they took their afternoon break, Grace said: "Kyle, there's something I want to talk to you about. Do you have time for us to go outside for a few minutes?" Kyle nodded.

"During the meeting today, it really bothered me that you said you had to help me finish the project, especially when I had already completed it when you asked me what I'd been working on," Grace told him. (**"I" phrase**) *While I appreciate that you were trying to help, when you said that it made me feel devalued."* (**understanding, "I" phrase**) Grace spoke assertively and tactfully, maintained eye contact, and presented a confident demeanor by standing up straight and allowing her hands to fall naturally at her sides.

Grace then kept quiet and allowed Kyle time to respond. He looked up and away from her, as though he was replaying the events of the meeting in his mind. Then he looked at her and said: "Sorry. But when you told me what you were working on, I'd already completed a project like that. I just wanted to let you know how I handled it."

Step 3: Define the Problem

"Okay," Grace said. "So even though I didn't ask for help, you thought you needed to help me."

"Yeah," Kyle admitted. "When I did that project the boss was very pleased with my work."

"But again, even though I didn't ask for help, you thought you needed offer your input?" Grace asked.

Kyle shrugged his shoulders and nodded. "I didn't mean anything derogatory by it."

Step 4: Offer Your Best Solution

Grace threw him an olive branch. "Look, Kyle, I appreciate that you're intelligent and are very good at what you do. I hope you appreciate that I'm also intelligent and know what I'm doing. I've been on the job for three years, and I'm proud that I'm good at what I do. When the boss assigned the project to me, he did so because he was confident that I'd do a good job. *Because I don't want to continue to feel devalued when you offer input, I'd like for us to resolve this.*" (**compromise**)

She continued. "*I'd appreciate it in the future if you respect that I know what I'm doing. I'd also like to know I can count on you when I need help, but unless I ask, I'd like to be able to complete my projects by myself without your input.*" (**compromise**)

Kyle didn't say anything. He looked a little peeved.

"*Can you agree to that?*" Grace asked. (**compromise**)

Step 5: Agree on the Resolution

Grace smiled warmly, and Kyle's look softened. "Yes, of course I'll agree to that. I'm sorry I've made you feel devalued."

"*Thank you,*" Grace said. "*I'm glad we talked this out because I do respect you, and I wouldn't want anything like this coming between us.*" (**resolution, reconciliation**)

Why This Works

Grace could have kept quiet and continued to put up with Kyle's superior attitude, but she'd had enough and knew it was time to speak to him.

By thinking first, then speaking assertively and respectfully, she had a constructive conversation with him. When she took the time to compliment Kyle on his job knowledge, he was more open to agree with the compromise she offered. While Grace understood that Kyle wasn't going to change his personality, she was pleased that he agreed to change his behavior toward her.

Something to Think About

Consider that the know-it-all may display this personality trait because of a deep-seated insecurity and lack of confidence. Some people who feel inferior try to act superior as a defensive mechanism. If you suspect this is the case, tread lightly, compliment your coworker when you can, and try to help him or her gain confidence.

Applying the Approach

Apply the following principles when dealing with a know-it-all:

- If it doesn't cause you a problem, it may be best to ignore the behavior.
- If the person's behavior starts getting on your nerves, it's time to directly confront your coworker so that you can resolve the conflict.
- Think and plan how you can assertively speak up and tactfully let the coworker know you don't need the help or unsolicited advice.
- Let the coworker know how the behavior makes you feel.
- Define the problem and ask the coworker if he or she understands how you see it.
- If you reach a stalemate after offering a compromise, compliment

the know-it-all on what he or she does particularly well, as this will usually change this person's attitude toward you.

- Reiterate that you also know what you're doing.
- Add that if you do need help, you'll be sure to ask for it.
- After gaining agreement on your proposed solution, offer phrases of resolution and reconciliation.

How to Deal with a Late-Nick

Holly was growing increasingly upset with her coworker, Sarah, who continually arrived late for work. Once again this morning, Sarah came rushing to her desk, but what really annoyed Holly was that Sarah had made an appointment with a customer. When he asked for Sarah, Holly introduced herself, apologized, and explained that Sarah hadn't arrived yet. The customer was clearly peeved. Holly didn't feel it was proper to make him wait for Sarah to rush in, so she handled his claim. To make matters worse, Sarah didn't even apologize to Holly, but rather brushed if off with a joke when Holly said something. Holly began to wonder if Sarah felt that the rules were made for everyone but her. Now that her lateness had affected a customer, Holly was more than irritated.

Some people are habitually late. Like Sarah, they feel that time constraints don't pertain to them. They show up late for dinner, fail to pick you up on time, and run into work late every morning. When these behaviors become habitual, these late-nicks can really bug you. You do a slow burn when once again they arrive late. You feel they aren't respectful of others or perhaps feel their time is more valuable. You may or may not speak up, but if you don't stop the behavior, you're likely to continue to do a slow burn.

When a coworker repeatedly shows up late for work, you have a right to speak directly to that person, especially if you're required to do his or her work. But, first try to figure out why the person is a late-nick, as that will help you determine how to structure your conversation. Does she have too much on her plate? Is she stressed to the max? Is he the type of person who doesn't like to live by rules? If the person has too much on her plate and is under a lot of stress, you'll handle the conversation more delicately you would with a person who feels that rules are made for everyone but him.

Sarah usually made a side comment that she thought she left home early enough to arrive on time. So, after thinking about the situation, Holly concluded that Sarah couldn't accurately judge time and wasn't leaving early enough. But when Holly had to handle Sarah's customer, that was the last straw. The lateness needed to stop.

Step 1: Think First

Holly was tired of hearing the same excuse, so she decided the best way to handle the conversation would be to let Sarah know how the lateness was affecting her. She also planned to offer a suggestion that could help her arrive on time.

Step 2: Gain a Better Understanding

The next morning, when Sarah rushed to her desk and said she thought she had left early enough, Holly said: "Sarah, you say the same thing every day. *I manage to make it on time every morning, and it bugs me that you're coming in late every day, especially since I had to handle your customer yesterday. I don't think that's fair."* (**"I" phrase**)

"I'm sorry, Holly. I think I'm leaving early enough. Maybe the clock here is different than at home."

Step 3: Define the Problem

Holly smiled and nodded, raising her eyebrows in understanding. *"Sure, if your clock is different, that could be the problem."* (**understanding**)

"But since you missed your appointment with your customer yesterday, it affected how I started my day, and that's a problem for me. **("I" phrase)** Can you see where I'm coming from?"

"Well that only happened one time. I don't see that it's a big deal," Sarah countered.

"Look, Sarah, it happened one time, but if you continue to come in late, it's likely to happen again. I just want to know that you understand where I'm coming from," Holly said.

Sarah replied: "I do. I said I'm sorry you had to handle my customer."

Step 4: Offer Your Best Solution

"Can I offer a suggestion that could help?" **(compromise)** Holly was happy that she had thought through the conversation beforehand and was prepared to offer a suggestion.

"Sure," Sarah said.

"Why not set your home clock 15 minutes early? That way you should have no trouble getting here on time. **(compromise)** *In fact, I like to arrive a little early as it helps me start my day much more relaxed,"* Holly added. **("I" phrase)**

Step 5: Agree on the Resolution

"That should help," Sarah said. "I'll reset all my clocks when I get home, so tomorrow you should see me arrive on time!"

"Excellent! **(resolution)**. *I think you'll find that arriving on time will help your day start off more calmly,"* Holly told her. **(reconciliation)**

Why This Works

Holly could have continued to do a slow burn whenever Sarah arrived late, but after handling a potentially irate customer, she decided to confront her and offer a suggestion to help Sarah get to work on time. Holly could also have complained to her boss, but she thought a better approach was to speak to Sarah directly. After all, if someone had a problem with her, Holly would rather hear about it from a coworker. After thinking about the prospective conversation, Holly decided to speak up the next time Sarah rushed in late. She was able to get Sarah to understand how her coming in late was affecting her and how it also affected a customer. Holly was prepared to offer a suggestion, which Sarah took to heart. Holly was pleased that she spoke up and that Sarah understood that her lateness was a cause of concern to her coworker.

Something to Think About

If one of your coworkers is consistently late to meetings and the meeting leader waits for the person to arrive before starting, you can try using peer pressure to handle the situation by making comments to the person when he or she arrives. Or ... you can speak to the meeting leader and let him or her know that your time is valuable too. If the coworker is habitually late, then it's up to the leader to speak to that person. The bottom line is to show respect for all attendees. Unless the tardiness is due to uncontrollable circumstances, meetings should always begin at the appointed time, whether or not everyone is present.

Applying the Approach

Apply the following principles when dealing with a late-nick:

- Don't suffer in silence. If someone's lateness affects you or your customers, speak up.
- Be sensitive to any personal issues that may be causing the problem.
- Explain to the person how being consistently late affects you.

- Make sure the late-nick understands why this is a problem.
- Be prepared to offer a workable suggestion that will help the person get to work on time.
- If the problem persists and it continues to bother you, you can either learn to ignore it or take the matter to your boss.

How to Deal with a Loudmouth

Becky was at her wit's end. She felt her blood pressure rising as her coworker, Eric, once again spoke to his customer as though he was talking in a wind tunnel. Becky was attempting to handle a customer's complaint on the phone, but had a difficult time shutting out Eric's voice. To make matters worse, her customer commented that she wondered how Becky could concentrate with all that noise. Becky replied that it was indeed difficult. She managed to get through the call and gave Eric a perturbed look, which he ignored.

It's hard when you're the unlucky one who works near a loudmouth. These coworkers talk so loud you have trouble hearing yourself think, not to mention trying to speak with your customers. As with Becky, matters are complicated when your customers hear the loudmouth and comment on it. Loudmouths' voices travel through the workplace as though they are speaking through a bullhorn. In addition to talking loudly, they may whistle, chew, move, or breathe loudly as well. To sum it up, working near a loudmouth can be hard on your ears. And loudmouths probably aren't even aware of the decibel level of their voices.

Depending on your workplace, you can try wearing earplugs or listening to a white noise machine. But how practical is that approach? Most likely not very, especially if you speak to customers or need to converse with coworkers. Let's face it: you need your ears! So how do you handle a loudmouth? Giving a perturbed look may work. Or, it may not. Saying "shh" may also work. But if you're at your wits end and feel your blood pressure rising whenever the loudmouth speaks ... or whistles ... or chews ... or moves ... or breathes, you need to speak up and handle the problem. Keep the focus on yourself, on how you have a difficult time concentrating and on how it's difficult for you to do your job. If customers have commented, you can also use that as back up.

Later that day, when Becky again had difficulty hearing a customer, she stood, faced Eric, and whispered through gritted teeth: "Will you please speak more quietly?" Eric looked at her with an annoyed expression and then gave her the brush off signal with his hand, letting her know that she was interfering with his ability to pay attention to his customer. Becky decided she had to take Eric aside and talk to him about her problem.

Step 1: Think First

Becky liked Eric, so she didn't really know what to say. But she knew that she needed to speak up because he didn't seem to understand how loudly he spoke. She thought about how to approach him without making him mad or defensive. She played through the conversation in her mind and then decided she was ready to have the conversation.

Step 2: Gain a Better Understanding

Becky waited until they were both off the phone and said: "Eric, do you have a minute?"

"Sure, Beck, what's up?" Eric smiled openly. Becky's heart sank because she didn't like confrontation, especially with someone she liked.

"Well, this is hard for me to say, Eric, but you talk so loud I have trouble hearing my customers. *It's become really difficult for me to concentrate on my calls.*" (**"I" phrase**)

"What? No one else seems to have a problem," Eric countered

Becky offered: "Well, actually, some of my customers do. Just this morning another customer commented that she could hear you."

Eric became defensive. "And some of my customers probably hear you too. None of our coworkers seem to have a problem with me."

Becky smiled sincerely. "I've never talked to our coworkers about this. *Eric, I'm sure you don't realize how loudly you speak.* (**understanding**) *But sometimes I do have trouble hearing my customers over your voice. And when they comment to me that they can hear you I know it's not just me being overly sensitive.*" (**"I" phrase**)

Eric said, "I didn't realize that I spoke that loud."

Step 3: Define the Problem

Becky was relieved that Eric no longer seemed defensive. *"I know you don't speak loudly on purpose.* (**understanding**) *And, I hope you understand that when I have trouble hearing my customers it causes a problem."*

He nodded and smiled. "I understand, and I can see how that would cause a problem."

Step 4: Offer Your Best Solution

Becky continued: *"I'd like to find a solution that we can live with. If we both try to speak more softly we should have no problem hearing our customers. How does that sound?"* (**compromise**)

Step 5: Agree on the Resolution

Eric joked: "As long as you promise to hold it down, I'll agree." They both laughed.

Becky said: *"I promise.* (**resolution**) *And no hard feelings, okay? You're so much fun to work with I wouldn't want to change that."* (**reconciliation**)

Eric said: "I feel the same way!"

Why This Works

After standing and whispering to Eric to be quiet, his offhand response made Becky realize that he wasn't aware that he spoke so loud that it disturbed her concentration. After thinking about how best to handle a conversation with him, Becky began by saying how hard it was for her to even speak to Eric about this. Then, she stated clearly how his loud voice was affecting her ability to hear her customers. She was able to give a concrete example from one of her customers that helped Eric understand the problem. Even though Becky knew that she didn't speak loudly, she compromised and included herself in the proposed solution that they both speak more softly, and Eric readily agreed. Becky was happy that she finally had the nerve to speak up about the issue and proud of the manner in which they resolved the conflict.

Something to Think About

Before confronting a loudmouth, make sure your coworker doesn't have a hearing impairment that may be causing the problem. If that's the case, be sensitive when approaching him or her. In fact, you may want to discuss the situation with your boss rather than the coworker and jointly determine the best way to resolve the issue to avoid embarrassing the coworker.

Applying the Approach

Apply the following principles when dealing with a loudmouth:

- Consider that loudmouths may not realize they're causing a problem for their coworkers.
- First try gently "shh-ing" the coworker when he or she interferes with your ability to hear your customers.
- If that doesn't work (and it may not), your next step should be to speak to the coworker.

- Think first about the best approach to take with your coworker, who may not realize he or she is interfering with your ability to hear. Explain that it's tough for you to concentrate and hear the person with whom you're speaking.

- Be prepared to offer examples, such as a customer commenting on the loudness.

- Use tact when speaking to your coworker, as the person may become defensive.

- Assure the person that you're the one having the problem, and then offer your best solution.

- If the problem continues after speaking to your coworker, you may have to ask your boss to move you to a quieter location.

How to Deal with a Meeting Monopolizer

Ben groaned when he thought about the afternoon's schedule. As the team leader, he ran the weekly staff meeting, which he had come to dread because he knew that Jason would hop on his soapbox and dominate the conversation, as he did during every meeting. As a result, meetings ran longer than they should and, more importantly, other team members clammed up because they just wanted the meetings to end. But what bothered Ben the most was that in the last meeting someone blurted out a rude comment, which caused Jason to say something rude in return.

Meeting monopolizers make you want to avoid meetings all together. They may interrupt someone who's speaking, drone on about an issue, go off on a tangent that isn't relevant to the meeting, or ask too many questions. These people love to talk; they also love to hear themselves talk. They feel that whatever they have to say is so important that it needs to be said, even if they take over the meeting by doing so and hold the other attendees hostage while they go on and on and on.

The bottom line is that meetings may be a part of your work schedule, but your time is too valuable to have them last overly long—especially when that's due to one of your coworkers talking too much. There are a couple ways to handle someone who monopolizes meetings. You can start by using peer pressure. Try joking by saying something like: "Jason, it's time to come up for air and let someone else talk. From now on, twenty words or less!" Everyone will laugh at the "joke" and hopefully the coworker will get it. But what if he doesn't? Or, what if he becomes defensive, as Jason did in the last meeting? Then it's up to the person conducting the meeting to deal with the issue. If that person is you, it's best to deal with it at the start of the next meeting before the monopolizer gets going.

Ben didn't want a repeat of the rude banter that occurred in the last meeting. He knew he'd have to say something to stop Jason's behavior.

Step 1: Think First

Ben decided the best approach would be to set some ground rules at the beginning of the meeting. He also felt it was important to address what happened during the last meeting. Ben didn't feel there was any reason to belabor the point with all the attendees by trying to gain a better understanding as to why Jason was monopolizing the meetings, so he planned to open the meeting by defining the problem. Because he had rehearsed what he planned to say, he spoke assertively. He also paid attention to his body language. He sat up straight, made eye contact with all the team members as he spoke, and his tone of voice conveyed confidence.

Step 2: Gain a Better Understanding

Not applicable, as explained in Step 1.

Step 3: Define the Problem

Ben thanked the team members for coming, then said: "Before we begin this meeting, I think we need to address what happened last week. Jason,

I want to apologize if we offended you in any way. *I'm sure what was said was meant as a joke, and I hope you understand that.*" (**understanding**) He looked directly at Jason as he said that. Then, as he continued, he made eye contact with each person: "*And we all need to respect each other since we have a time commitment for our meetings. It's important that everyone has the opportunity to share ideas and not feel left out.* ("**I**" **phrase**) Would you all agree that's important?"

Ben looked at each attendee, and when they all had nodded or voiced agreement, he continued.

Step 4: Offer Your Best Solution

"*After the last meeting, I came up with a solution I'm positive will work. First, I want each of you to have a chance to contribute. So going forward, I'd like everyone to hold their comments until I finish presenting each issue on the agenda. At that time, I'll go around the table and ask each of you for your input. That way everyone will have a chance to contribute. But ... I also brought a timer. I've thought about how much time is realistic and decided that each of us, including me, will have two minutes to address each item. This way, we'll stay on target and get through the meetings in a timely manner. How do you feel about doing that?*" (**compromise**)

Ben waited for a response, which was positive from the team members. He then looked at Jason, who nodded in agreement. But then Joe spoke up. "I'm thinking about the two minutes for each of us to speak. There's usually 10 of us at the meeting. If we all have something to say, it'll require 20 minutes for each item. I think you should have two minutes to present the item, but I think one minute for the responses should be adequate."

"How does everyone feel about one minute to respond?" Ben asked.

After a short discussion, the attendees were in agreement that one minute would be doable.

Step 5: Agree on the Resolution

Ben then said: *"Great! I'm glad we're all in agreement. I'm confident that this approach will work and that we'll get done with our meetings quicker."* (**resolution**)

The meeting ran smoothly, and the team members seemed to enjoy the timer approach. Before adjourning the meeting Ben said: *"I want to thank each of you for respecting our time. I'm glad we were able to work this out in a respectful manner."* (**reconciliation**)

Why This Works

In this situation, there was no point in taking Jason aside to try to gain a better understanding as to why he was monopolizing meetings. The problem affected the rest of the attendees, so Ben decided that opening the meeting by defining the problem and then offering a compromise to set new ground rules was the best approach. By addressing the problem and offering a solution, everyone was able to discuss and reach an agreement. This made everyone feel valued. Because he maintained his confidence, Ben also gained respect as a leader who didn't ignore problems.

Something to Think About

But what if you're not the meeting leader? What if the meeting leader doesn't speak up? If the extra time added to the meetings is beginning to affect your productivity and you have a tough time getting your work done, you have to deal with the problem. Now your issue is with the person running the meetings, so speak up and explain how it affects you. Work through the five steps to resolve the conflict. And be prepared to offer suggestions and discuss ways to resolve the problem.

Applying the Approach

Apply the following principles when dealing with a meeting monopolizer:

- If you're not conducting the meeting, try politely interjecting a comment to let the person know that you have something to say.

- If the offender is a coworker who continuously monopolizes every meeting, you may try taking a humorous approach to let the person know it's time to be quiet.

- If you are the meeting leader, you might politely interrupt the monopolizer and say something like: "That's a good point. I'd like to hear how everyone else feels."

- Understand that this approach most likely isn't going to work long term and that it's best to address the issue directly.

- At the beginning of your next meeting, define the problem. Gain the attendees agreement that they understand.

- Offer a compromise by setting meeting ground rules that limit everyone's time to contribute.

- Make sure that everyone buys into the compromise and proposed solution, which most likely the other attendees will. Or, in the case above, a discussion about an alternate solution may ensue. Just be sure to gain agreement on the best solution.

- It's also important to gain agreement from the offender.

- Then stick to your guns. If the person tries gaining control of the meeting, remind the person of the ground rules everyone agreed to.

How to Deal with a Mistake Maker

Anna was tired of fixing Ryan's mistakes. Ryan is fairly new, but he received the same training that Anna did when she was hired, and she didn't make as many mistakes when she was new.

Like Anna, you may be tired of cleaning up other people's messes, and it can get tiresome very quickly if you're cleaning up the same person's messes. Then, you have to wonder: Does your coworker suffer from a lack of training or a lack of motivation? Before jumping on the problem and speaking to your coworker, analyze the situation.

Is your coworker new? Has he been properly trained? Has your boss followed up to make sure he's doing the job correctly? If you determine that your coworker needs additional training, you may decide to help by offering to be his mentor. Tell the person you understand what it's like not to feel fully comfortable with job duties and that you'll be happy to be the go-to person for any questions he has.

But suppose your coworker has been trained. She's attended the same training classes that you have. She should know the job as well as you, but she continually makes mistakes. After thinking about the situation, you conclude that she always seems scattered. Has something happened in her life recently? Is she on stress overload because of home responsibilities? Or, is she simply not that committed to the job? When you take the time to try to figure out what's going on in her life, you may gain insight that will help you direct the conversation.

Anna didn't know much about Ryan personally, so she couldn't draw any conclusions that might help determine whether he needed additional training or just didn't care.

Step 1: Think First

Anna decided it was time to speak up about Ryan's tendency to make mistakes. However, before she approached him, she took the time to analyze the situation. Because she didn't know enough to determine the cause of the mistakes, she'd need to draw the reasons from him. Anna waited for a time when they'd be alone before approaching Ryan.

Step 2: Gain a Better Understanding

On their way back from lunch, Anna said: "There's something I've been wanting to talk to you about. *I want you to know that I understand what it's like to be the new kid on the block and feel out of your comfort zone.* **(understanding)** *What I wanted to talk to you about is that this week I've fixed three errors you made on orders and that's caused me to get backed up with my own work. Right now I'm feeling a little overwhelmed."* **("I" phrase)** She smiled sympathetically, made eye contact, and conveyed concern with her facial expression.

"Geez, I'm sorry about that," Ryan said sheepishly.

"No need to apologize," Anna responded "*I just wanted to talk to you so we can figure out what's going on and see if I can help you.* **(compromise)** Each of the errors had to do with assigning the correct dispatch codes."

"I admit I'm struggling with that," Ryan told her. "There are so many codes to remember and it takes too long to look them all up on the computer, so I'm trying to go from my memory. I guess that's the wrong approach."

Step 3: Define the Problem

Anna nodded to show she understood and said: "So what's happening is that you're trying to remember them all, which can be pretty much impossible. *I remember feeling exactly like you do. I didn't think I'd ever learn them all. But over time I've learned most of them. And you will too."* **(understanding)**

Ryan nodded in agreement.

Step 4: Offer Your Best Solution

"How does this sound?" she continued. *"I'll be happy to make up a quick reference sheet with the more common codes.* **(compromise)** You can

keep that handy, and you'll only have to check the computer for the ones that we don't typically deal with. In fact, there are times I still have to do that myself." They both laughed.

Step 5: Agree on the Resolution

"Wow! That would be a huge help," Ryan said. "I appreciate that you talked to me about this rather than going to the boss."

"*Of course!*" Anna replied. "*I'm glad that I can offer something that'll help you.* (**resolution**) As I said, *I fully understand what it's like to be the new kid on the block.* (**understanding**) If you have any other questions, don't hesitate to come to me. *You'll catch on in no time. I'm happy to help you feel more comfortable here.*" (**reconciliation**)

Why This Works

Anna didn't want to continue fixing Ryan's mistakes, but before she confronted him, she took the time to think about the situation from Ryan's perspective. This helped her empathize with how it felt being new. During the conversation, she displayed concern through her body language and facial expressions. She spoke in a direct manner, citing the specific types of mistakes she had to fix. Anna showed that she was truly interested in finding out what was causing the errors. When Ryan stated that he was trying to go from memory, Anna suggested a compromise by offering to make up a quick reference for him. Ryan appreciated that she didn't go directly to their boss. Because Anna demonstrated that she cared and was trustworthy, these two coworkers will develop a close working relationship.

Something to Think About

This scenario had a positive ending because Ryan was receptive to the conversation. But what happens if your coworker becomes defensive when you mention that you've had to fix multiple problems? In that event, keep your cool. Assure your coworker that you're trying to resolve the problem. Provide details about the errors. It might help to remind your coworker that you came directly to him rather than to the boss. "Look, I didn't go over your head on this. *I'm coming to you so that we can figure out what's going on and how we can stop this from happening in the future.*" **(compromise)** Hopefully, your coworker will calm down enough to discuss the issue, and you can move through the five steps to resolve the conflict. But if the coworker continues to be defensive and refuses to discuss it, refer the problem to your boss the next time it happens. Just make sure you have your documentation when you do that.

Applying the Approach

Apply the following principles when dealing with a mistake maker:

- Don't confront the person until you've analyzed what's causing the problem.
- Be specific, and provide examples of the errors you've fixed.
- If necessary, ask questions to better understand.
- Together, define the problem.
- If you discover it's a training issue, offer to show the correct procedure.

- If your coworker is new, offer to mentor.
- If you feel that it's caused by a lack of motivation to do the job correctly, address the problem with your coworker and explain how the mistakes affect you. Give the coworker the chance to explain. Try to reach a compromise. If that doesn't work, seek help from your boss and be prepared to provide specifics.

How to Deal with a Negative Nelly

Susan avoided Mike at all costs. Mike was a negative Nelly and Susan, a positive person, couldn't stand listening to him complain about anything and everything. Whenever she saw him in the hall, she pretended to answer her cell phone. Whenever he walked toward her work station, she picked up the phone and pretended she was making a call. Still, Mike managed to corral Susan whenever she didn't see him coming. And once he started his complaining, there was no turning off the switch. Susan had learned that making upbeat comments had no effect, so she stopped trying to get Mike to see things from a more positive perspective. Being negative was so engrained into his personality, that's all Mike seemed to understand.

Negative people can really bring you down, and rarely, if ever, will you be able to bring them up. Like Mike, some folks are wired with a negativity gene and every time they open their mouths you can guarantee that something downbeat and depressing will come out. For these people, something is always wrong. And to a positive person, that becomes tiring quickly. The truth is that it's tough being around negative people, especially if you view the world through rose-colored glasses.

Perhaps you've tried unsuccessfully to cheer up your negative coworker. You may have tried to get him to see the situation from your positive perspective. Or, you may have countered her negative rant with an uplifting response. Most likely, you've been met with more negativity. So don't try to get this person to see the world from your vantage point.

Just as it's difficult for you to understand the negativity, it's equally as difficult for the negative Nelly to understand your cheeriness. The best way to deal with a negative Nelly may be, like Susan, to avoid the person at all costs. But you also know that may prove impossible when it's a coworker with whom you interact on a daily basis. If you can't learn to ignore the negativity, then speak to the person. Tell him or her how the negativity affects you. Be prepared to offer specific examples. Empathize with the person, but stress that all that negativity brings you down and you're not willing to listen to it any longer.

Susan had enough of Mike's negativity, so she decided to let him know she was no longer going to be a willing participant in listening to his constant moaning and groaning.

Step 1: Think First

Susan wanted to handle her conversation with Mike in a way that would end well, and she didn't want to anger him. She only wanted him to understand how his negativity was affecting her and make it clear that she really didn't want to hear to it any longer.

Step 2: Gain a Better Understanding

The next time Mike came into her workstation, Susan didn't pretend to be on a phone call. Rather, she sat up straight and made eye contact. When he started his negative rant, she said: "Excuse me, Mike, but there's something I need to say. *Every time you speak to me it's to complain about one thing or another, and it's really getting to me. All the complaining brings me down.*" (**"I" phrase**)

Mike replied: "Wow! That came out of nowhere."

Susan realized he took her comment the wrong way, so she softened her approach. "Look Mike, I like you. I like working with you. *And I empathize with you that you'd like some things to change around here.* (**understanding**) *I'd like some things to change too. But I don't* *think that complaining is going to make things better. In fact, for me complaining makes them worse because I'm focused more on what's wrong than on what's right. And there are a lot of things that are right too."* **("I" phrase)**

Mike countered, "Well yeah, I agree with you. But there's a lot of stuff going on that bugs me."

Step 3: Define the Problem

Susan was prepared for his negative response and took the opportunity to define the problem. "So do you feel that complaining about them is going to change things?"

"No, but when something bugs me I have to get it off my chest," he said.

"Okay. So you have to get things off your chest and that's why you complain to me?"

Mike shrugged his shoulders. Susan stayed silent, looked at him, and waited for him to say something that demonstrated he understood. After an uncomfortable silence, he said: "I guess so. I don't like keeping everything bottled up inside."

Susan didn't back down: "But do you understand how all the negativity is affecting me?"

"You made that clear," Mike responded. "I'm sorry if I've been a downer."

Step 4: Offer Your Best Solution

She continued to maintain a confident demeanor and made eye contact when she said, *"As I mentioned before, I really do understand where you're coming from.* **(understanding)** *And I'm glad that you understand that I don't want to fill my day with negativity. Can we agree to keep our conversation on neutral topics?"* **(compromise)** Susan smiled at Mike and gave him an understanding look.

Step 5: Agree on the Resolution

Mike smiled and nodded. "Sure."

Susan added: *"I'm glad you and I can agree to that.* (resolution) *The way I view work is that I have to be here eight hours a day and I need to keep my mood positive; otherwise I'd go home in a bad mood every night. Thanks for understanding."* (reconciliation)

Why This Works

This was a tough conversation for Susan because she knew Mike wasn't going to change his personality and suddenly view the world more positively. But she also wasn't willing to continue having him bring her down every time they spoke. So she decided to tell Mike point-blank that she wasn't willing to listen to his complaining, but she wanted to say it in a way that wouldn't offend or anger him. Susan kept a confident demeanor and made eye contact when she spoke to Mike. She told him how his negativity brought her down, was able to define the problem, and got him to admit that he didn't like keeping his feelings bottled up. When she reiterated that she wasn't willing to listen to all the negativity and offered a compromise that they keep their conversations on neutral topics, Mike had no choice but to agree, and Susan quickly followed up with phrases of resolution and reconciliation.

Applying the Approach

Apply the following principles when dealing with a negative Nelly:

- Your best approach may be to ignore the negativity.
- Don't try to cheer this person up. It won't work.
- Don't allow a negative Nelly to affect your attitude.
- If you can, avoid the negative Nelly at all costs.

- Take your break and eat lunch at a different time, which may help you avoid entering into conversations.

- If can't avoid this person, then speak up.

- State how the negativity brings you down.

- Confidently tell the person you're not willing to listen to all the complaining.

- Be prepared to cite examples if the person denies being a constant complainer.

- Make sure the person understands how the negativity is affecting you, as this will help the negative Nelly understand that it's causing you a problem.

- Offer a compromise by assertively saying that you want to keep your conversations on neutral topics.

- It may help to empathize with the person, but be very clear that you aren't willing to continue listening to the complaining.

How to Deal with a Personal Hygiene Offender

Vanessa has bad breath. In fact, some days her breath is so bad her co-workers dread being near her. Unfortunately for Claire, she doesn't have much choice since she occupies the desk next to Vanessa's. She's tried facing the other way, keeping her distance when speaking to Vanessa, running a small fan facing in Vanessa's direction, and spraying a room deodorizer, yet her coworker hasn't taken the hint. Claire likes Vanessa and doesn't know how to approach the subject. She doesn't want to hurt her feelings, so she keeps her distance.

Personal hygiene offenders take many shapes and forms. If the offender is wearing unkempt or stained clothes to work or has oily hair or dirty fingernails, it may be best to let your boss deal with it. But when the problem affects you, why endure it? If it's caused by an offensive smell, such as bad breath, body odor, or excessive perfume, and you're unwilling to put up with the offending odor, it's best to say something.

This is probably the touchiest subject to address because you're talking about someone's personal hygiene. Although you'll learn to address the issue tactfully, unless you feel confident speaking to the person it may be best to talk to your boss and let him or her handle the situation. If you do decide you're up to having the conversation, don't make a big deal out of it. Tactfully state what you've noticed and be respectful if the person becomes embarrassed or defensive.

The next morning, Claire noticed that one of their coworkers put a bottle of mouthwash on Vanessa's desk and then laughed with others. Claire removed the bottle before Vanessa saw it. She mulled over speaking to her boss about this, but felt that if the situation were reversed, she'd rather hear about it from a coworker than her boss.

Step 1: Think First

Claire thought about how to handle the situation and felt so uncomfortable she almost talked herself out of having the conversation. But she kept coming to the same conclusion: If the situation were reversed, she'd want to know about it, especially if some of her coworkers were laughing behind her back. So she decided to take the plunge and speak to Vanessa, yet handle the conversation in a very sensitive and thoughtful manner.

Step 2: Gain a Better Understanding

When they were walking to their cars after work, Claire decided it was a good time to speak up. "Vanessa, this is such a tough subject for me to address, but lately, I've noticed an odor coming from you that I'm sure you're not aware of. I think it might be your breath. *I'm concerned about the impact this may have on our coworkers and customers, and it's affecting me.* (**"I" phrase**) *"I hope you understand that I'm coming to you as a* *friend. If the situation were reversed, I'd rather hear it from you than someone else."* **(understanding)**

Vanessa looked mortified. "I'm so embarrassed. I had no idea."

Claire said: *"I hope you realize that I'm telling you this because I care about you.* **(understanding)** I don't like having this conversation, but after thinking about it, I know I'd want someone telling me."

"Oh yes," Vanessa said. "I agree. I have a tooth that's been bothering me, and I have a dentist appointment next week. I wonder if that's the cause."

Step 3: Define the Problem

Claire nodded, maintaining a concerned look on her face. "If you have a tooth that's bothering you, that very well could be the reason for the problem with your breath." Claire felt they were in agreement about the cause of the odor so she moved to the next step.

Step 4: Offer Your Best Solution

"I'm sure your dentist will be able to figure out what's causing it," Claire offered. **(resolution)** She was relieved that Vanessa hadn't become defensive. She hadn't offered a compromise, but she didn't feel that was necessary. She reinforced the resolution that Vanessa had a dentist appointment and felt there was no need to prolong this step of the conversation.

Step 5: Agree on the Resolution

Vanessa hugged Claire, and then covered her mouth when she spoke. "I'm really glad you came to me about this."

Claire responded: *"Me too. I care about you and even though this was really difficult for me, I felt it was best that I speak to you about it. I know I'd want someone to speak to me if I had a problem I wasn't aware of."* **(reconciliation)**

Why This Works

Confronting someone about a personal hygiene issue is very difficult. But speaking to Vanessa was a much more respectful solution than taking a passive–aggressive measure, such as anonymously putting mouthwash on her desk. Claire handled the situation tactfully and respectfully. She didn't make a huge deal out of it, but candidly addressed what she had noticed and stated that the odor was affecting her. When Vanessa became embarrassed, Claire offered a positive assurance. Because Claire conveyed that she was speaking to Vanessa out of concern, they were able to move through the conversation with Claire reassuring her that seeing the dentist the following week would most likely result in a successful outcome.

Applying the Approach

Apply the following principles when dealing with a personal hygiene offender:

- If the problem is due to someone's appearance and it doesn't affect you, ignore it.

- If the problem is caused by an unpleasant odor, such as body odor, bad breath, or too much perfume, it's best to speak to the person directly—if you're comfortable having the conversation.

- If you don't feel comfortable speaking to the person, then by all means take the issue to your boss.

- If you decide you're able to have the conversation, be prepared for the person to become embarrassed or defensive.

- Remain calm and offer a positive assurance that you're speaking out of concern.

- Define the problem as it affects other people and try to get the person to take ownership.

- Then offer a suggestion that might alleviate the problem.
- At the end of the conversation, offer a phrase of reconciliation and reiterate that you care about the person and that's why you're speaking to him or her about it.

How to Deal with a Personal Space Invader

Bob cringed whenever Stan came around because he'd move in so close he made Bob uncomfortable. Earlier today, when Bob was speaking on the phone to a customer, Stan hovered over him, waiting for him to finish. Bob became so unnerved he lost his train of thought and had to place his customer on hold to ask Stan what he wanted. Bob had enough of Stan's personal space invading, but he didn't really know how to handle the situation.

We all have a comfort level when it comes to proximity and personal space. Standing about two feet from another person is generally considered a safe distance, but some people don't seem to understand the rule. They stand too close, get in your face, and hover over you when you're seated. They're not doing this to annoy you. They just don't have proximity boundaries. Touch can be another form of personal space invasion; some people aren't comfortable with someone touching them. Patting someone's hand, putting an arm around the person, or any other form of touch that's done to enhance communication may be offensive to the receiver.

The best way to handle a personal space invader is through body language. Often, if you back up when someone gets too close, they'll back off a bit. The same goes for people who pat your hand or put their arm around you. If you back away, they should get the message. If they don't, then it's time to say something.

At the same time, if you find that people with whom you're speaking are continually backing up or leaning away from you, you're probably guilty of being a space invader and need to back off a little. Pay attention to other people's body language and be careful not to get in anyone's space! And always keep your hands to yourself.

Bob always backed up whenever Stan got too close, but Stan didn't get the message. Bob liked Stan and felt uncomfortable telling him to back off.

Step 1: Think First

Bob decided the best way to speak to Stan was to make a joke of it. That way he felt he wouldn't offend Stan or hurt his feelings. Close proximity was comfortable for Stan. It wasn't for Bob.

Step 2: Gain a Better Understanding

The next time Stan got in his space, Bob said: "Hey Stan, you'd better stand back a bit. I ate garlic for lunch." He held his hand over his mouth and waved his other hand up and down as though trying to get rid of the odor. But then Bob realized this was a temporary fix, and he quickly decided that the best approach was honesty. He couldn't feign a garlic lunch every time Stan got too close.

So he added: "Actually, I didn't have garlic for lunch. *The truth is that I'm not comfortable standing so close.*" (**"I" phrase**) Then he made a sweeping arm gesture and laughed. "I seem to have this invisible force field, and it's just about an arm's length."

Stan said: "Geez, I didn't realize I was doing that."

"Oh, I know that. You're just more comfortable being close to people than I am." (**understanding**)

Stan looked mortified. "I'm sorry, Bob."

Step 3: Define the Problem

Bob felt bad since Stan truly didn't seem to know he was invading his space. "No need to apologize. I'm the one with the issue, not you. I just hope that you understand where I'm coming from."

"Oh sure," Stan said.

Step 4: Offer Your Best Solution

Then Bob added: "*It's just that I'd appreciate it if you'll stand a little farther from me. That'll make me feel a whole lot more comfortable.*" Bob's comment was made in a joking manner to let Stan know he was taking responsibility for having the problem with closeness. (**compromise, "I" phrase**)

Stan laughed with him but then grew serious. "Has anyone else said anything?"

Bob shook his head. "No, I've never discussed it with anyone. Hey, we all have different comfort levels so I may be the only one who needs my space. *I don't want to offend you but I felt it was important to say something. Hope you're okay with it.*" (**compromise**)

Step 5: Agree on the Resolution

Stan nodded. "Sure! I'll be more mindful of that and keep a little more distance between us."

Bob laughed, then added: *I'm glad we talked about it. And thanks for understanding.*" (**resolution, reconciliation**)

Why This Works

This is a tough subject to bring up because the space invader isn't deliberately doing anything to annoy you. Some people are just more comfortable being close to others. Since Stan didn't get the message when Bob backed up and moved away from him and since it bothered Bob, he did the right thing by bringing it up. Bob liked Stan, yet when he joked about eating garlic, he immediately realized that wasn't the best approach. So, he addressed the issue directly and honestly. By taking responsibility for not being comfortable with closeness, Bob didn't embarrass Stan and they were able to end the conversation on a positive note.

Applying the Approach

Apply the following principles when dealing with a personal space invader:

- If you back up, space invaders may realize they're too close.

- If someone pats your hand, slowly pulling back your hand will send a message that the touch is unwanted.

- Similarly, if someone puts an arm around you or hugs you, backing away will send a clear message.

- If these measures don't work and the person continually invades your space, you'll either have to accept the proximity or speak up.

- If you decide to speak up, taking responsibility for the discomfort may be the best tactic to use in getting your point across and not embarrassing the person.

- Define the problem as it affects you. Joking about your need for distance may alleviate any discomfort or embarrassment the other person may feel.

- Offer a compromise and ask for agreement.

- Be sure to end the conversation on a positive note, either by joking about your need for distance or, as Bob did, thanking the person for understanding.

How to Deal with a Slacker

Lydia and Tom have worked together for three months. He transferred from another office and even though he was as experienced as she, Tom hasn't been doing an equal share of the work. He has such a fun personality that at first Lydia didn't mind pulling the extra weight. But lately it's started annoying her that she's doing more than her fair share of the work.

Do you work with someone who always manages to fly under the radar? If you do, your coworker is likely a slacker. The biggest problem in dealing with slackers is that they're usually likeable people. They're easy going and fun to be around. That's part of their charm. But they also have a knack for avoiding work and responsibility. They look like they're working when, in fact, they're doing nothing constructive. These are the people who don't volunteer for projects and then come up with good excuses for avoiding them. These are also the people who are very good at convincing others that they're pulling their weight.

Slackers may even fool the boss. They may think they're clever, but to deal with this type of worker, you're going to have to be a little cleverer. When the boss asks for volunteers for yet another project, you could suggest that the team members discuss their current projects so that everyone will know who's able to take on another one. This is a great way to make the slacker come clean. When everyone states what they already have going on and the slacker can't honestly take credit for the same amount of work, it'll be clear who should take on this project.

But if you don't have the opportunity to make the slacker take responsibility and it's bugging you that you're doing more than your fair share of the work, you're going to have to confront the slacker directly. Don't expect your coworker to come clean and immediately change his or her ways, though. You can expect slackers to evade, dodge, or weasel their way out of the conversation. You'll have to plan how you want to confront this person, have concrete data to present, and then stick to your guns when discussing the situation. Remember that people who fly under the radar are very good at what they do!

Lydia joked with Tom about his doing less work but so far he just keeps shuffling papers on his desk and spending his time staring at his computer. She began to suspect that he was staring at the same screen! Since they're a two-person operation, Lydia decided it was time to speak with Tom about her problem.

Step 1: Think First

The biggest problem was that they had become close friends, even socializing outside the office. Lydia didn't really know how to tell Tom it was time he pulled his share of the workload, but she also knew that's exactly what she needed to say. She didn't want to compromise their friendship, but on the other hand she was beginning to feel used and was even wondering how much her friendship meant to him if he thought his behavior was acceptable. After thinking about how she wanted to proceed with the conversation, Lydia felt confident confronting Tom.

Step 2: Gain a Better Understanding

"Hey Tom, something's been bugging me, and it's time we talk about it," Lydia said.

"Sure, Lydia, what's going on?" Tom said, looking concerned.

"Well, I don't really know how to say this other than to say it directly," she replied. *"Frankly, I'm doing most of the work and that's not fair. I hadn't said anything about this because I don't want anything to affect our friendship, but lately I've felt a little used."* (**"I" phrase**) Lydia had a hard time maintaining eye contact, but every time she found her eyes straying, she brought them back to look at Tom. She looked concerned and that's exactly what she felt.

Tom looked shocked and said, "Whoa, wait a minute! Why would you say such a thing? You can see that I'm working just as hard as you are."

"Yes, I can see that you're working," Lydia told him. (**understanding**) "But I have the productivity reports for the last three months on my desk, and I'm completing almost double the orders that you are. I'll be happy to show the report to you."

"I didn't realize that I wasn't pulling my fair share," Tom said, looking upset and a little miffed.

Step 3: Define the Problem

Lydia showed him the report, then spoke softly, hoping to calm Tom down. "Tom, I'm not coming to you to upset you. From what I'm gathering, you thought you were doing your fair share of the work."

"Of course I did," Tom replied adamantly, "until now."

"Then you can see by the report that you haven't been."

"Yeah, the numbers don't lie. I thought I was doing more than I actually was."

Step 4: Offer Your Best Solution

For a moment, Lydia wanted to end the conversation right then, thinking that everything would be all right. But she reminded herself that unless they agreed to a resolution, he might not change his behavior and she'd end up becoming even more upset.

She continued: "Look, Tom, I value our friendship, but I also value our working relationship. I'd like for us to do an equal share of the work. *I do have a proposal that I think will be fair. How about if we divide up the daily orders first thing in the morning rather than taking them from the pile throughout the day? That way we'll both know what we're facing each day and, if either of us gets backed up, we can help each other."* (**compromise**)

Step 5: Agree on the Resolution

"Well, I guess that'll work," Tom agreed, reluctantly

Lydia could tell that Tom wasn't thrilled with the arrangement but since he had agreed to it she didn't back down. *"Great!"* she said. *"I'm so glad we worked this out.* (**resolution**) *I wouldn't want anything to come between our relationship—both on and off the job."* (**reconciliation**)

Why This Works

Confronting a slacker is difficult when the person is likeable. It's even more difficult when the coworkers are friends like Lydia and Tom. During their conversation Lydia almost backed down, but she was glad she didn't. That would have only upset her more because nothing would have changed. Lydia knew she had to stick to her guns, so she presented concrete facts to back up her claim of doing double the work. She proposed a solution and, when Tom reluctantly bought into it, Lydia seized the moment to gain his agreement for the resolution. She'll have to continue to monitor Tom's workload because slackers aren't usually keen on the idea of actually having to do their share of the work, but he agreed to her solution so it'll be easier for her to stay on top of the workload going forward.

Applying the Approach

Apply the following principles when dealing with a slacker:

- Don't be lulled into inaction because you like the slacker and want to believe it's going to be okay.
- Focus on the amount of work each team member is producing.
- Don't try to shame or goad a slacker into doing more work. These types are masters at evasion and aren't easily shamed.
- Speak to the slacker about the production inconsistencies.
- Before you do, run through the likely conversation in your mind. Prepare yourself for the slacker not to take responsibility. This person isn't easily changeable.
- Stick to your guns, especially if you like the slacker. State that you appreciate your friendship but that you also value your working relationship.
- Share concrete facts that support your claim.
- Offer a compromise.
- When the slacker takes the bait, even if reluctantly, jump on it. Thank the slacker for agreeing to your proposal.

- Continue to monitor the situation to make sure the workload is evenly shared.
- If it isn't, it may be time to involve the boss.

How to Deal with a TMI'er

Paige enjoys working with her coworkers ... except for Allie, who is extroverted and gregarious to the point that she divulges way too much information (TMI) about herself. Paige has asked her coworkers how they feel about Allie and most are in agreement that they could do without hearing every little detail about her life. Two of the team members, however, encourage Allie to share what's going on in her love life and then joke about her behind her back. Paige feels uncomfortable knowing how they encourage her for the purpose of laughing at her. It's gotten to the point that she doesn't even want to be around the group when Allie lets her loose lips yammer.

People who disclose too much personal information are usually harmless. They're sociable, friendly folks who don't seem to understand there's a fine line between saying enough to hold an interesting conversation and revealing too many details about their personal lives. And, although most coworkers feel uncomfortable hearing overly personal and private details about one's life, as in Allie's case, some on the receiving end may encourage the TMI'er and then joke about the person afterward.

However, when in a work setting, stay on the high road. When the person starts talking, you can try joking by covering your ears and saying "TMI." But if that doesn't stop the person from flapping their lips, do the right thing. Take the person aside and have a heart to heart. Let the person know that a line was crossed, and you're uncomfortable hearing all the details.

If you realize you may be a TMI'er, take this advice to heart. Stop! Remember that when you're at work you should always maintain a level of decorum and professionalism. Think before you speak and share only what you'd share with your mother ... or a child ... or a stranger.

Paige was no prude, but she found that her coworkers' and Allie's be-
haviors were beginning to bother her. She felt that whether they were en-
couraging Allie to tell them about her love life or were joking about her
behind her back, none of them were behaving professionally. She thought
about how to handle the situation and decided the best approach would be
to speak with Allie directly.

Step 1: Think First

Paige understood that Allie was just trying to fit in with the team and
didn't know that she was being talked about and laughed at behind her
back. Paige felt the best approach would be to handle this situation delicately since Allie was a likeable, friendly person whose behavior was
meant to be harmless. Paige wanted to protect Allie's dignity, yet get her
to understand she was divulging way too much information.

Step 2: Gain a Better Understanding

When Paige approached Allie, she spoke politely. "Allie, rather than taking our break with the group, would you mind if we took it together? I'd
like to talk to you about something."

"Sure. Is everything all right?" Allie looked concerned.

Paige smiled warmly. "Sure. *I just want to talk about something that's*
a little uncomfortable for me to say in front of the team. (**"I" phrase**) I
really don't know how to say this other than to just say it. *Allie, I under-*
stand that you're friendly and outgoing, but it seems that you're revealing
too much information about your private life to the team members. (**un-**
derstanding) *A couple of them are continuing to talk about it when you're*
not around and that's making me uncomfortable because I don't think
they're being fair to you. (**"I" phrase, understanding**)

Allie offered an explanation. "I'm a very open person, and I just
don't see a problem with talking about my personal life. But who's doing
that? I don't want anyone talking about me behind my back."

Step 3: Define the Problem

Paige nodded and showed concern in her facial expression. "I don't want to cause a rift among our team and really, it isn't important to know who's continuing your conversation when you're not around. From what I'm gathering, you feel very comfortable talking about your private life to us."

Allie said, "Well yeah, until now!"

Paige continued: "Then you realize how saying too much may not be a good thing?"

"I sure do," Allie responded.

Step 4: Offer Your Best Solution

"I'd like to offer a suggestion that I'm sure will work for you. When you're at work, just don't divulge the nitty-gritty. Save those details for your close friends; you know, people outside of work," Paige offered. **(compromise)**

Allie said, "Well now I'm embarrassed that I've already told too much."

Paige answered respectfully. *"I'm not telling you this to make you feel embarrassed. Can I tell you how many times I've said things that I later regretted?* **(understanding)**

"But how do I change?" Allie asked. "Everyone's used to having me tell them about my dates."

Paige thought for a moment before responding. *"Going forward, when someone asks you about a date, just say it was good. If they encourage you to share the details, tell them there's not much to say. Now if you saw a movie or went out to dinner, talk about that. Just stop before you say anything you wouldn't want your mother knowing. How does that sound?"* **(compromise)**. Both women laughed.

Step 5: Agree on the Resolution

Allie nodded. "I get it. Just stick to the G-rated stuff."

Paige added: "Or PG! *I'm glad we talked this out.* **(resolution)** *I like you a lot and so do the rest of our team members. Please don't think anyone was saying anything hurtful or spiteful about you. They're probably just a little jealous that your life is more exciting than theirs."* **(reconciliation)**

Why This Works

Paige could have spoken to the team members who were talking about Allie behind her back but realized that doing so wasn't going to stop Allie from sharing too much information. Allie was the person she needed to speak to, but Paige felt uncomfortable tackling a delicate subject. Throughout their conversation, Paige spoke respectfully and was able to convey the importance of maintaining professionalism at work. Adding that the coworkers were likely jealous ended their conversation on a lighthearted note.

Applying the Approach

Apply the following principles when dealing with a TMI'er:

- If someone you work with is sharing too much personal information, first try covering your ears and saying "TMI." This often clues the person in to the problem.
- You can try letting let the information go in one ear and out the other.
- If that doesn't work and you find it difficult to transition from that conversation back to work, then it's time to talk to the person.
- When planning your conversation, be extremely tactful and respectful because this person isn't aware of giving way too much personal information.
- The person may become embarrassed so offer words of understanding.
- When the person understands that this behavior is a problem, your next step is to offer a solution by suggesting he or she refrain from telling too much.

- End the conversation on a positive note to help the person over any embarrassment.

How to Deal with a Whiner

Alex sat next to Mary, whom he silently called "Whiney Wendy." Mary whined her way through each day. Nothing seemed right in Mary's world. Whether it was her child, husband, boss, or another coworker, Mary seemed to think that someone was out to get her or was doing something on purpose to irritate her. Alex was tired of listening to her whining and had tried getting her to view situations more objectively, but that approach hadn't worked. He also tried changing the subject but that, too, hadn't worked.

Nothing ever seems right in the world of a whiner. Unlike a negative Nelly, who views the world negatively and complains about everything, a whiner turns the negativity inward to focus on how it affects them. Whiners whine because it gives them a good feeling and may ease their frustration. But it gives those around them anything but a good feeling, and it will certainly raise the frustration level of anyone within earshot.

Dealing with a whiner can be trying because whining is a part of their personality. You can't change the person, but you can change your reaction to the whining. You've most likely already figured out that trying to get a whiner to view a situation more objectively falls on deaf ears. The truth is that most whiners really don't want anything to change. They just like the reinforcement whining gives them. So if you're able to, learn to ignore it. Tune out the whiner when he starts complaining. But you know that may prove difficult, and the whining is apt to get to you at some point. The best approach may be to empathize, listen to the complaint, and then take a problem-solving approach by helping her find a solution. Handling the conversation this way will get the point across that you're not just going to sit by and listen to the whining without expecting the person to also come up with a solution.

Alex decided to take a problem-solving approach. He hoped that by asking Mary to offer a solution about how to handle her whining, she'd get the message that he wasn't willing to sit silently and listen to her continual carping.

Step 1: Think First

Alex thought about how to address Mary the next time she whined and decided the best way would be to head her off at the pass as soon as she started whining. He planned to tell her point blank how her complaining was affecting him, but mainly he planned to stop her in her tracks by asking her to offer a solution to each problem.

Step 2: Gain a Better Understanding

He didn't have to wait long to test his new tactic. Right after lunch, Mary said: "Our boss once again proved she has no respect for me. While we were gone, she dropped more work on my desk. How am I supposed to input all these bills when I haven't finished the ones from the morning?"

Alex quickly responded: "*Oh wow. I can relate to how you feel.* **(understanding)** How are you going to handle the situation?" Mary looked at him with a bewildered gaze. Alex felt he was on the right track to put a temporary stop to her whining.

"What do you mean how am I going to handle the situation? What can I do? I have all this work and now she's dumped more on my desk."

Step 3: Define the Problem

"Complaining about it isn't the answer. The way I see it you have two choices. You can explain to her what you already have going on or you can do the work." Alex spoke with confidence, maintained eye contact, and held a neutral facial expression.

"I wouldn't feel comfortable telling her I have too much work, even though I do."

"Hey, I understand you have a lot to do. We all do," Alex said. **(understanding)** "Look, I haven't said anything before, but actually we both have a problem. Your not telling her you have too much work is creating a problem for you, *and frankly, when you complain to me, it's a problem for me because all the complaining brings me down."* **("I" phrase)**

Mary continued to look confused. She wasn't used to Alex speaking to her like that. Finally, she said: "I didn't realize I was causing you a problem."

"Look, Mary, I'm only trying to help you out," Alex told her. "When you allow her to dump work on your desk it's obviously causing you a hardship. **(understanding)** *And when you tell me about it, I have trouble refocusing on my work because it's upsetting to me too."* **("I" phrase)**

Mary nodded in understanding. "I see where you're coming from."

Step 4: Offer Your Best Solution

Alex explained: *"You can either do the work or you can talk to her and let her know how much work you already have."* **(compromise)**

Mary spoke hesitantly. "I suppose I can try to get it all done."

"If that's the case, then if you don't mind, please don't complain about it to me," Alex said, looking at her sympathetically. **(compromise)**

Step 5: Agree on the Resolution

"I won't."

"Thank you," Alex said. **(resolution)** *"I'm glad we talked this out, and I'm also glad you came up with a solution that'll work for you."* **(resolution, reconciliation)** Alex looked down at the bill he was working on and found it hard containing his smile. He was more than pleased with the way he handled Mary's whining and planned to use this approach every time she started complaining.

Why This Works

As long as Alex was a willing participant by listening to Mary's whining, nothing was going to change, because she really wasn't looking for things to change. Alex's approach worked well because he made a plan to confront her the next time she whined and ask what she planned to do. Then, he made sure he explained the problems it created for both of them. He followed up by explaining possible solutions. When Mary said she thought she could get all the work done, Alex quickly affirmed her resolution and offered a phrase of reconciliation.

Applying the Approach

Apply the following principles when dealing with a whiner:

- At first, ignore the whining. If the whiner gets no response from you, he or she may take the whining elsewhere.

- But if ignoring it doesn't work and the whining is getting to you, then do as Alex did and head the whiner off at the pass.

- Respond to the complaint with a phrase of understanding.

- Ask what they're going to do about the problem. This sends the message that you're expecting them to come up with a solution.

- If the person doesn't come up with a solution, explain the problems the whining causes for both of you.

- Be prepared to offer a solution.

- Most likely the whiner will back down, and when they do, quickly affirm the solution and offer a phrase of reconciliation.

How to Deal with a Wimp

Nicole overheard one of her coworkers ask Kim, another coworker, to finish a project because she was overloaded with work. Kim sighed and said: "Sure, put it on my pile." The coworker replied: "Great! Thanks a bunch, Kim. You're the best." Nicole knew that her team members often took advantage of Kim's passiveness, so she walked over to Kim and said: "You should learn how to speak up for yourself. Everyone takes advantage of you

and it isn't right." Kim shrugged her shoulders and shook her head resign-
edly. Nicole walked back to her desk, but Kim's wimpy behavior continued
to bother her, mainly because she liked Kim and resented the way others
took advantage of her.

Telling wimps to change their behavior would be like telling infants to
get up and walk. Until they're ready and able, they're not capable of doing
it. Like Kim, some people are hard wired to be passive, shy, or mousy. They
don't know how to stand up for themselves. They allow others to walk all
over them. They comply with the wants and needs of other people. They
allow other people to interrupt them. And, they wouldn't think of speaking up or asking for help. They may also be overly empathetic, to the point
where they value other people's feelings over their own.

The best way to help a wimp is to teach the person how to be less
wimpy and more assertive. Telling someone to speak up for themselves,
without communicating helpful ways to do that, will have little or no effect
on a wimp. When Kim shrugged her shoulders and shook her head re-
signedly, Nicole walked back to her desk knowing that unless Kim learned
how to say no, her coworkers would continue to take advantage of her.

After thinking about what she had said by telling Kim she should learn
to speak up for herself, Nicole realized that she could be more helpful by
taking a different approach.

Step 1: Think First

Nicole decided to ask Kim if she'd mind allowing her to be an "assertiveness" mentor. She truly wanted to help Kim and felt that she could do
that by teaching her different phrases to say when their coworkers tried
to take advantage.

Step 2: Gain a Better Understanding

Nicole said: *"Kim, earlier this morning, when I said you should learn how*
to speak up for yourself, I realized I spoke out of turn. **("I" phrase)** *I know*

that it's difficult for you to say no whenever anyone asks you to do some-thing, even when you know they're out of line." (**understanding**)

"That's true. I just don't know how to say no, and I end up being taken advantage of. Sometimes it bothers me, but I don't know what to do about it," Kim replied.

Step 3: Define the Problem

Nicole replied: "So you'd agree that when people take advantage of you, it creates a problem for you?"

"Definitely," Kim replied. "I wish I could be more like you."

"And you understand that it's a problem for me, too, because I don't like seeing that?" Nicole said

"I appreciate that," Kim said.

Step 4: Offer Your Best Solution

Nicole nodded, maintained a concerned facial expression, and smiled warmly. *"If you don't mind, I'd like to help you."* (**compromise**)

"I wouldn't mind at all," Kim said.

"I'd like to suggest some phrases that work well for me, and I know they'll work for you as well. (**compromise**) Here's one that always works. When someone asks me to do something and I already have my plate full, I say something like: 'I'd like to help you out but I've already got more work than I can handle today.' I've found that saying that does the trick because it lets them know that my time is important too."

"That's a great suggestion. I'm going to try it next time." Kim said, seeming determined.

Step 5: Agree on the Resolution

Nicole then said: *"I'm glad you don't mind me helping you out."* (**resolution**)

"If you can teach me how to stand up for myself, I won't mind in the least!" Kim told her.

Nicole added: *"Terrific. Learning how to say no is tough, but once I learned the value of that word I gained a lot of confidence and was able to stand up for myself. I care about you and if I can help in any way, please don't hesitate to ask."* **(reconciliation)**

Why This Works

Once Nicole realized that she took the wrong approach with Kim, she reassessed how to handle the conversation. After they agreed on the cause of the problem, she asked Kim if she could help her become more assertive. When Kim readily agreed, Nicole was prepared and gave her an example of an assertive phrase. But Nicole also knows that changing one's behavior takes time, so she plans to pay attention and continue to mentor Kim, helping her become more assertive and confident.

Applying the Approach

Apply the following principles when dealing with a wimp:

- Rather than telling the person he or she should change, take a different approach and ask the person if you can help them learn to be more assertive.
- Guide them to understand why not being able to say no can create a problem. In addition, explain that it's a problem for you because it bothers you to see them taken advantage of. Then offer to teach some assertive phrases.
- Assure the person the phrases work because they've worked for you.
- Don't overwhelm the person. Start with one example, and build from there.
- Maintain the person's self-esteem by acknowledging that learning to say no is difficult, but that it can be done.

5

Powerful Phrases for Challenging Situations with Your Boss

Throughout your career, you'll probably work for many bosses. Because no one is perfect, the good bosses will have some challenging personality traits, quirks, and habits, while the bad bosses will have some redeeming qualities. One thing is certain: whether you consider your bosses good or bad, you're going to like some things they do and dislike others. When something bothers you, you'll need to decide whether to ignore the behavior or speak up. If you choose to say something, confronting your boss is going to be quite different than confronting a coworker. Let's face it: your boss has the upper hand and an advantage over you. He or she may hold the purse strings that pay your wages and keep you employed. That isn't to say that you should put up with bad behavior, but that you need to approach the situation with more sensitivity and tact than you might when speaking to one of your peers.

This chapter describes ten challenging personality types of bosses. For each type, you'll learn how to use the five-step conflict resolution process to speak to your boss about challenging situations. Sample scenarios are included that will help you resolve conflicts successfully. As in the first four chapters, the powerful phrases are denoted in *italics* with the type powerful phrase noted in (**bold**). For each of the behaviors, a "Something to Think About" helpful tip is included as well, demonstrating how to handle an unusual or difficult situation. When you become comfortable applying the five-step process, you'll develop the confidence to effectively communicate with any type of boss for whom you work.

Basic Rules When Confronting Your Boss

When discussing a problem situation your boss, speaking calmly and confidently can increase your ability to make your feelings known in a constructive, nonthreatening manner. Focusing on the facts and offering a positive solution will enable you to keep the conversation productive. If you first view the situation from your boss's perspective and understand his or her personality, you'll have a better idea of how to deal with the situation. When you're able to successfully resolve problems with your boss, you'll develop a stronger, more trusting, and supportive relationship with each other.

Before learning how to handle the various personality types, here are some basic rules to remember when attempting to resolve a conflict between you and your boss:

- Only approach your boss when you feel certain that you'll be able to maintain your confidence and assertiveness throughout the conversation.
- When speaking to your boss, use positive and constructive language.
- Always remain calm, no matter how your boss speaks to you.
- Always treat your boss with respect.
- No matter what happens during the conversation, never insult your boss or other members of upper management.

- Clearly state the facts when telling your boss what's bothering you and how it made you feel.

- Be prepared to share examples.

- Offer your compromise and focus on how you can work together to solve the problem.

- If you feel it's impossible to have a productive conversation with your boss, speak to someone else who can provide guidance about how to deal with the problem.

- Don't ever burn your bridges; you never know when you'll have to cross one again.

Bear in mind that it may be in your best interest to rule on the side of caution and learn how to put up with your boss's quirks, idiosyncrasies, and personality traits. If you can ignore or work around your boss's negative habits and keep your focus on doing a good job, you'll have an advantage in being able to maintain a calm, confident demeanor. But if something bothers you to the point that it affects your work or your attitude, then it's time to speak up.

The following 10 examples involve conflicts between an employee or a group of employees and the boss, in which the employee or employees have made the decision to discuss the matter with him or her. If your entire team has a problem with the boss, the group should discuss the best way to handle the problem before entering in a conflict resolution meeting. As you'll see in the examples, the best approach is often to have one person assume the role of the spokesperson for the group with the other members of the team in attendance.

How to Deal with an Abusive Boss

Brandon was busy stocking shelves when his boss, Matt, came up behind him. "What are you doing? You're stocking those wrong. I thought you knew what you were doing but evidently you don't. Do I have to show you again how to do it right?" Brandon was upset that Matt berated him in front of a customer, who looked dumbfounded and uncomfortable witnessing the situation. Brandon was used to Matt's put downs and negative reinforcement, but he really didn't like being called out in front of customers. Brandon shook his head and said: *"I'm sorry. I know you like the items touching, and I'll take care of it."*

Some bosses have no tact and use no discretion when voicing their opinions to employees. Like Matt, when they see a problem, they abusively criticize or reprimand the employee in front of customers rather than taking the employee aside and discussing the matter privately. They manage only through negative reinforcement. An abusive boss is never satisfied, is overly critical, uses intimidation techniques, and speaks in threatening tones. In other words, this type of boss is a bully.

As you learned in Chapter 4, no one has the right to bully another, even when the bully is your boss. Working for an abusive boss is tough, but the bottom line is not to take it personally. It's likely your boss treats everyone this way. It also could be that your boss acts this way because someone higher up on the totem pole is treating him or her that same way. However, that doesn't make the boss's behavior okay, and it's best to address any abusive situation when it occurs. Stand up for yourself, and tell your boss how you want to be treated. Just do it in a tactful, respectful manner. Calmly and assertively explain how the abuse made you feel. Present yourself as the voice of reason when you speak. Cite one or more examples. If, like Brandon, customers were nearby, explain to the boss that you noticed they looked uncomfortable overhearing the conversation. Then tell the boss how you'd like to be treated in the future. When you speak with confidence, you'll be perceived as someone who respects yourself and expects to be treated well.

Sitting idly by and allowing a bully to heap abuse on you is never good. It can affect your work, your state of mind, and even your health.

If the situation continues to be unbearable after speaking to your boss, go to a higher authority or discuss the situation with a human resources manager. Just make sure you have documentation about the abuse to back up your claim.

Brandon was tired of being called out in such an abusive manner, especially since a customer was present. He was proud that he had kept his cool with Matt but wanted the abusive behavior to stop.

Step 1: Think First

Brandon was also a little intimidated by Matt's overbearing mannerisms. He tried to analyze why Matt thought that abusing his employees was all right and concluded that Matt was the type of boss who never had anything good to say to or about any of his employees. When he saw something he didn't like, he didn't appear to have the filter to know when it was best to delay the conversation. Rather, he launched into speaking his mind, no matter how he spoke or who else was present. Brandon had seen him berate other coworkers, yet knowing he wasn't the only one who was treated abusively didn't make it right. When he felt confident that he'd be able to speak assertively and say what he wanted to say, he approached Matt in his office.

Step 2: Gain a Better Understanding

"Matt, do you have a minute? I wanted to talk to you about something." Brandon spoke assuredly, made eye contact, and stood up straight.

Matt nodded without smiling. "I have a lot of work to do, so keep it short, okay?"

Brandon said: "I wanted to talk to you about what happened this morning when you told me I was stocking the shelves wrong. *A customer was within earshot and she heard every word, which made me very uncomfortable.*" (**"I" phrase**)

"Hey, I saw what I saw, and you were stocking the shelves wrong. What did you want me to do, let you continue?" Matt spoke gruffly.

Brandon thought before he spoke, and then said: *"I understand that, Matt. You saw me doing something wrong so you wanted to correct me,* (**understanding**) whether or not you did it in front of a customer."

"What difference does that make?" Matt asked.

Brandon was prepared for that sort of glib comment. "To me it does make a difference."

Brandon sensed that Matt's facial expression conveyed some understanding about how he felt so he moved into defining the problem.

Step 3: Define the Problem

"I apologize that I wasn't stocking the items butted against each other. I know that's not how you like it. But when you were speaking to me, the customer looked very uncomfortable. And, I already mentioned that I felt uncomfortable with her being present. That's the issue I wanted to talk to you about."

Matt said: "Okay. Go on."

Step 4: Offer Your Best Solution

Matt took a deep breath before offering a compromise. *"I'd prefer, if you have to correct me about something I'm doing, that you do it out of earshot of others.* (**compromise**) As for what happened this morning, I'd have appreciated if you waited until the customer walked away. Or, you could have called me aside and spoken to me."

Matt nodded: "I'll try to remember that."

Step 5: Agree on the Resolution

"Thanks," Brandon responded. (**resolution**) *"And I'll do my best to remember how you like each item stocked on the shelves."* (**reconciliation**).

Why This Works

Brandon knew that he wasn't going to transform Matt from being an abusive bully into a courteous, tactful boss, but he also knew that he needed to say something to let Matt know how he felt being berated to in front of a customer. Because he practiced the conversation in his mind and only approached Matt when he felt confident, Brandon was able to speak assertively and get his point across. He took responsibility for not stocking the shelves properly and apologized for not doing his job to Matt's liking. Then he offered a compromise and explained exactly how he wanted Matt to speak to him in the future. Matt really had no other choice but to agree with Brandon's proposal. Brandon felt good after the meeting, during which both men kept the conversation rational and calm.

Something to Think About

If your boss is normally a reasonable person who recently said something to you that was abusive, think about what may have caused your boss to behave badly. Is your boss under a lot of pressure? Did something happen recently that could affect your boss's attitude? It could be a personal problem or perhaps your boss's boss has said something that caused him or her to behave badly. So think before speaking up. You may decide to let it go, but if it continues to happen speak up. Doing so may give your boss a much needed sounding board.

Applying the Approach

Apply the following principles when dealing with an abusive boss:

- It's always best to speak up when the abuse happens, as Brandon did, but first take the time to think how to handle the discussion.

- Speak in specifics, and cite an example of the abusive behavior. Then state how it made you feel.

- If customers were within earshot, it will make your case stronger to let the boss know that the behavior likely made the customers feel ill at ease.

- An abusive boss isn't likely to back down immediately, so when you define the problem don't expect an empathetic comment.

- Offer your best solution by explaining your compromise in very specific terms. State exactly how you want similar situations to be handled going forward.

- When you speak with confidence and state your case assertively, your boss is more apt to agree with your request.

- If the same behavior happens again, calmly remind your boss of the agreement you had reached.

- If you continue to accept abuse, that's the best you can hope to receive.

How to Deal with a Controlling Boss

Jessica was busy working on a project when her boss, Sam, walked into her cubicle. "Here's a project I need you to complete. It's due on Friday," he said, dropping the project on top of the project she was currently working on and walking away without saying another word. Jessica picked up the project and threw it to the side, although she really felt like throwing it in the garbage can. She was tired of Sam always telling her what to do. It bugged her that he never bothered to ask if she could handle additional work.

Some bosses seem to get stuck in a controlling style of management. It's easier for these types to tell you what to do than to ask. Controlling bosses come across as authoritative: it's their way or the highway. They feel they have the right to dictate and would never think of asking an employee for input. Do what they say, and don't challenge them. They would consider it beneath them to ask for their employees' suggestions or ideas. They like to make all decisions, even those that directly affect the team members. The bottom line is that they feel they know best, so why ask. After all, no one is as capable as they are and they won't hesitate to let employees know.

There may also be other reasons for the controlling behavior. It could be that he's overloaded with responsibilities and is so busy that he doesn't have the time to ask or enter into discussions, so he relies on telling employees what to do because it's easier and quicker. Or, perhaps she's a new manager, who hasn't yet found her comfort zone, lacks confidence, and feels that being authoritative and bossy will make her look more managerial. Your controlling boss may be very amiable, too. You like your boss; you just don't like the dictator-like actions.

So what do you do when you work for a controlling boss? It will be helpful if you can figure out why your boss acts like a dictator, as this will enable you to deal better with the behavior. If he's overly busy and stressed or if she's a new manager, you may decide to cut some slack and ignore the controlling behaviors. But if the controlling behavior becomes unbearable or upsetting to you, then it's time to sit down with your boss and have a heart to heart. Speak in specifics when you address the problem.

For the most part, Jessica had learned to ignore Sam's dropping work on her desk and walking away. She accepted that being authoritative was Sam's nature, so she did her job and tried to let his behavior roll off her back. She liked Sam and didn't feel comfortable telling him that he was giving her more than her fair share of work, so she had grown accustomed to taking the additional work without saying anything. But now she felt put upon. After all, it wasn't fair that he continued to pile on work just because he knew she was capable of getting it all done.

Step 1: Think First

After stewing about the latest project Sam had dropped on her desk, Jessica came up with a plan to ask for his help in prioritizing the work he assigned to her. She hoped that after meeting with Sam, he'd realize just how much work he had given her to handle. She also hoped to get the point across that she'd appreciate being asked before he dropped work on her desk. She took her planner and the pile of project folders and met with Sam in his office.

Step 2: Gain a Better Understanding

"Thanks so much for meeting with me," Jessica began, making sure her tone and facial expressions conveyed respect. She smiled warmly at Sam. *"The reason I wanted to speak with you is that I'm feeling a little overwhelmed, and I need your help in prioritizing my projects."* (**"I" phrase**)

She then laid out her planner on his desk and placed the pile of nine projects next to it. He raised his eyebrows, and his expression wasn't lost on her. It told her just what she had been thinking: Sam didn't realize the volume of projects he had dropped on her desk.

Step 3: Define the Problem

Jessica seized the opportunity to define the problem: "As you can see, I've got a lot of projects to complete. I have no problem with completing these. The problem I have, though, is that I'm not sure how to prioritize them. I'd like for us to review them and then you can tell me how you'd like me to prioritize each one. That way I'll get them completed to your expectations."

"I didn't realize how much work you have," Sam said, seeming surprised.

Step 4: Offer Your Best Solution

"Oh, that's okay Sam. I figured you didn't." (**understanding**) Jessica lifted the top four folders and said: "These are the ones I'm currently working on." Then she tapped the stack. "And these are the ones you recently gave me to work on that I haven't started."

Sam took the folders from her. Then he reiterated: "I really didn't realize I gave you this many to work on."

Jessica offered a compromise: *"Perhaps going forward, before you drop a project on my desk, do you think you could check with me to see what I'm already working on?* (**compromise**) That way I won't get in this bind."

Sam said: "Sure." Together they went through the projects. Sam said he'd reassign the five projects that Jessica hadn't yet started, and they prioritized the other four.

Step 5: Agree on the Resolution

"Thanks so much, Sam. I'm glad we agreed that you'll check with me before assigning work. (**resolution**) *I appreciate that you trust that I'll always do my best."* (**reconciliation**)

Why This Works

Jessica knew that being controlling was part of Sam's personality and that wasn't going to change. She had learned to ignore his bad habits, but when he continued to pile work on her, she spoke up. She also took a smart approach. Jessica never complained that she felt like a dumping ground. And she didn't say no to Sam or tell him that she couldn't handle all the work. Rather, Jessica took a problem-solving approach by asking for Sam's help in prioritizing the work he had assigned to her. Because Jessica stayed positive throughout their conversation, when she suggested that he ask before assigning a project, Sam readily agreed.

Something to Think About

If your boss is acting in a controlling manner because he's new, cut him some slack. Show him that you're a capable and supportive employee, which will help gain his trust. As his confidence increases, you're liable to see less of the controlling behaviors. But if not, talk to him about it. If you speak as a trusted employee who's trying to help your boss communicate in more productive ways, he should be receptive to the conversation.

Applying the Approach

Apply the following principles when dealing with a controlling boss:

- Do your best to ignore the controlling behaviors and focus on doing the best job you can.
- If your boss continually displays a behavior that affects your ability to complete your work or is giving you a negative attitude, then talk to him or her.
- Speak respectfully when you define the problem. Like Jessica, it'll be to your advantage to take a problem solving approach rather than sounding as though you're complaining.
- Explain specifically the problem you're having. Take responsibility that you're the one with the problem, not the boss.
- Then offer a compromise for how you'd like the situation to be handled going forward.
- Gain the boss's agreement and offer phrases of resolution and reconciliation.
- Then go back to doing the best job you can.

How to Deal with an Egotistical Boss

Rachel and her coworkers were mulling over the memo they received from their boss, Patricia, who scheduled an impromptu meeting later that afternoon to discuss the team's failure to win a district-wide sales contest. "Here we go again. It's always our fault," one of the coworkers complained with others chiming in. "Well, you'd think she'd be proud of us coming in a close second. But no!" "And if we did win, we still wouldn't get credit. Then it would be Patricia's achievement." "She's really great at taking credit for our accomplishments, and also great at blaming us when things don't go her way." Rachel nodded in agreement. Patricia was the type of boss who basked in the spotlight, but never accepted responsibility when things went wrong. Then, it was always someone else's fault. One of the team members shared that he overheard Patricia speaking to another manager and blaming the team for losing the contest. They were in agreement that once again Patricia wasn't going to take any responsibility for the loss.

If you work for an egotistical boss, then you may have nodded your head when you read the scenario above. Egotists love to take all the credit for team accomplishments but failures are never their fault. They'll easily pass the blame onto others without taking any responsibility as the team leader. These types of bosses are always looking out for their own best interests. And, they probably don't like the spotlight to shine on their employees because that takes attention away from them. They may even consider employees who do a great job a threat. Egotistical bosses don't bother to spend a lot of time with their employees, either. They're too busy or too involved with their own self-interests for too much employee interaction. The bottom line is that it's always about them.

If you work for a boss with a huge ego, it's going to be difficult to ignore the bad behavior. If, however, you can learn to do that, it'll make

your life at work much more enjoyable. Learn to play the game by staying on top of yours. Do your best job, and try not to take it personally
when you're blamed for something. When your boss takes an ego trip
and starts boasting about accomplishments, speak up about your contributions to her or his success. Whenever you have the opportunity, make
your contributions known to others. If you or your team achieves an
objective or surpasses a goal, write a memo to your boss (and copy
someone in upper management) to share the good news. In other words,
take some of the credit back whenever you can. Remember, too, that
people outside the group know that your boss is an egotist because egotists never try to hide their feelings. But if you do decide to speak to your
boss about a situation, start by describing the behavior and how it made
you feel. Make sure your boss understands the reason you're upset before offering a compromise. When you offer your compromise, speak
constructively so that your egotistical boss doesn't feel threatened or become angry.

*The team had grown tired of Patricia taking credit for team successes
but refusing to take responsibility for team failures. One coworker suggested that when Patricia started raking them over the coals, they should
speak up and tell her how they feel about her. Rachel was the voice of reason on the team, so she volunteered to be the spokesperson.*

Step 1: Think First

Rachel knew it was going to be a tough conversation with Patricia, who
wasn't likely to be receptive to hearing anything negative about herself. Rachel thought through various ways to handle the discussion and
decided to begin by stroking Patricia's ego. That would soften her up
enough so that Rachel could enter into a discussion about how the team
felt when she took all the credit for winning but never took responsibility for losing.

Step 2: Gain a Better Understanding

Patricia didn't mince words when she spoke to the group. "I want you to know how embarrassed I am to lose the contest. After all, last month my name was on top and that's where I always want it to be. I was humiliated at the conference when the district manager announced that another manager won. I don't ever want that to happen again."

Rachel felt a lump in her throat but she knew that it was now or never. She responded: "Patricia, I volunteered to speak for the team, and I want you to know how sorry we are to have disappointed you. We would never do anything on purpose to humiliate you."

"I was extremely humiliated. And I am very disappointed in all of you." Patricia looked around the room when she spoke.

Rachel said: "We also want you to know that we want your name to be on top because that means we're the top team."

Patricia's facial expression softened. She added: "I appreciate that all of you want to be the top team."

Even though Rachel wasn't completely convinced that Patricia understood where she was coming from, Rachel understood exactly where Patricia was coming from, so she moved into defining the problem.

Step 3: Define the Problem

Rachel said: "*We understand how much winning means to you.* **(understanding)** But we hope that you understand how much winning means to us as well."

"Of course," Patricia said flippantly.

Rachel added: "*Last month when we won the contest, you didn't give the team any credit and that really bothered us. Frankly, we felt unappreciated.* **("I" phrase)** We feel that everything we do, winning contests … or losing them, is a team effort. And as our leader, you're part of our team.

The problem we have is that we'd like you to share success with us, but also share responsibility when we don't succeed."

Patricia nodded. "I see where you're coming from."

Step 4: Offer Your Best Solution

Rachel wasn't sure if Patricia really understood her definition of the problem, but she thought that offering a compromise might help get the point across. *"What we're saying is that we're all in this together— with you—and we'd like for you to be in this with us too. We're one team. When we do well we'd like for you to acknowledge our contributions, and when we fail we'd like you to acknowledge that you're in this with us."* **(compromise)**

Patricia looked down at her papers and shuffled them. Then she looked to the group and nodded slowly. "I understand what you're saying. Last month, when we won the contest, you should have known that I was proud of you. Perhaps I should have said something."

Step 5: Agree on the Resolution

"Then going forward, you'll tell us when you are proud of us?" **(compromise)** Rachel asked.

"Yes, I'll be sure to tell you when I'm proud of you."

"And when we fail, we fail together?" **(compromise)**

Patricia nodded.

"Great. Thank you. **(resolution)** *Patricia, we want you to know that we like winning just as much as we do. We feel terrible that we lost this contest, and we promise to always do our best for you."* **(reconciliation)**

Why This Works

The discussion would not have had a positive outcome if the entire team had started voicing their complaints. Patricia would have felt she was being ganged up on and become defensive. Rachel handled herself well throughout the discussion. She began by stroking Patricia's ego and taking group responsibility for disappointing her. Then, she moved through the conversation quickly and assertively by defining the problem and offering a compromise that the team would appreciate being acknowledged by Patricia, who would have little choice but to agree. Even though the team knew that her egotistical manner wasn't going to change, they felt good about speaking up and addressing how they felt.

Something to Think About

If you suspect that your ego-driven boss acts that way due to insecurities, tread lightly. She may be acting egotistically to compensate for her own shortcomings. Offer compliments when you see her doing something well, and encourage her by offering suggestions as to how you'd like her to communicate with you and your team. Doing so may increase her confidence level and lessen her need to act egotistically.

Applying the Approach

Apply the following principles when dealing with an egotistical boss:

- Try to ignore the egotism and concentrate on doing your best.
- Showcase your achievements whenever there's an opportunity. Send an email, speak up during a meeting, or meet with your boss to discuss your accomplishments. While you might not feel comfortable shining the spotlight on yourself, it's in your best interest to take credit because your boss isn't likely to give you any.
- If you do decide to speak up, as Rachel and her team did, stroking your boss's ego a little may increase receptivity to the rest of the conversation.
- Make sure you clearly describe the behavior and how you felt.

- Don't expect your boss to suddenly understand or acknowledge the problem. If necessary, move into defining the problem, as that should enhance understanding. Then, you can state your compromise and work toward a resolution.

- Understand that your boss isn't likely to change her ways. The best you can hope for is that she listened and will change her method of communicating with you and your team going forward.

How to Deal with an Incompetent Boss

Jack worked for his company for six years as a sales associate. He was the most experienced member of his team of eight employees and was regarded as the mentor for his coworkers. When his manager, the company owner's brother, retired, Jack hoped that he'd be promoted, but that wasn't to be. Before retiring, his manager took Jack aside and told him that the owner was going to bring in his daughter, who had recently graduated from college, to take over the manager position. Jack understood the family dynamics of the company, but still he was disappointed to be passed over for someone who had no company on-the-job experience. To make matters worse, Hailey, the new manager, tried to act like she knew what she was doing rather than ask for help when it was clear to the sales team that she was not qualified to do the sales job, let alone to manage the team.

Working for someone who's incompetent can be frustrating. Your boss isn't qualified to do the job, yet she's in charge of your team. She may not have any managerial experience, yet she's your leader. Bosses who are incompetent are often poor communicators because they don't know enough about the job, the company, or the team to communicate effectively. They don't provide adequate training for obvious reasons. They're unable to make decisions, or they take too much time mulling over the best option. Often, they make poor decisions because they lack the job knowledge and insight about the company and team dynamics. Consequently, they may come across as being unfocused. As a result, this type of boss is an ineffective leader. And, there isn't much you can do about it.

When you work for an incompetent boss, learning how to adapt will make you more skilled and proficient. He may be new to the company and hopefully will receive training. Or, he may have been around a while but has no clue as to what you do or how to manage. In any event, if your boss isn't able to give you direction, you'll become more self-reliant. If your boss makes poor decisions, you'll become more confident initiating your own outcomes. In other words, your boss's lack of abilities could be a blessing in disguise. When you concentrate on how you can fill in the gaps for your manager, you'll develop important leadership skills. Rather than emphasizing your boss's lack of skills or complaining, try to help him or her improve by assisting and teaching. You'll gain the boss's trust and ultimately make yourself look good in the process. If you present yourself as a valuable, supportive employee who contributes to the success of your team, you'll stand out as a positive role model and leader.

Jack liked his job too much to allow Hailey's incompetence to get to him. After all, it wasn't Hailey's fault that her father put her in this position. But when Hailey made a poor decision that could affect Jack's appraisal rating and pay, he decided to speak up. Jack decided to take a proactive approach when discussing the effect of the decision by offering his help.

Step 1: Think First

Before he spoke to Hailey, Jack took time to think about her weaknesses. She had graduated with a degree in business management, and Jack felt that as her confidence grew, she'd develop her managerial and leadership skills. But Hailey lacked the technical job knowledge, which hindered her ability to make sound judgments and decisions. Jack believed he could help Hailey by offering to teach her the technical aspects of the job. He just wasn't sure how receptive Hailey would be, since she overcompensated for her weaknesses by acting like she knew how to do the job.

Step 2: Gain a Better Understanding

Jack stood in Hailey's doorway and asked: "Do you have a few minutes for us to talk about something?"

"Sure," Hailey answered. "Come on in, and have a seat."

Jack sat down and took a deep breath. Leaning forward, he said: "I wanted to talk to you about your decision to change the manner in which our jobs are assigned. This change is going to decrease my work load, which in turn could affect my appraisal rating and ultimately my paycheck. *I pride myself on being able to do more than my share of the work and taking some of it away will make me feel that I'd be contributing less than I'm capable of doing.*" (**"I" phrase**)

"I made the decision because I wanted to even out the workload," Hailey responded.

Step 3: Define the Problem

"*I understand where you're coming from,*" Jack replied. (**understanding**) "But the problem I have is that we don't all work at the same pace. Adding more work to some of the other employees could cause two problems. First, productivity may slip. Second, the work might not be completed to customers' expectations."

"I didn't think about that. I made my decision based on what I thought would be fair to everyone."

"I hope you understand the problems that decision could cause." Jack spoke confidently, making eye contact and continuing to lean forward.

"I do now," Hailey said.

Step 4: Offer Your Best Solution

Jack understood that he was taking a big risk with what he was about to say but he said it anyway, and he said it with sincerity. *"Look, I can understand how it must feel to be a new manager.* (**understanding**) *What I'd like to ask is that since I'm the most senior member of our team, I'd like to be involved with decisions that affect me and the team. And I'll be happy to help you with any job-related questions you have. If you'd like, I can teach you what we do."* (**compromise**)

"Okay. I'd appreciate some help learning the job. And yes, I do see where you're coming from. Going forward, I'll run things by you that I know will affect you."

Step 5: Agree on the Resolution

"Good. (**resolution**) *I felt a little funny approaching you about this but I know what it's like being new, and I'm more than willing to help you learn the job.* (**reconciliation**) We'll tackle that however you want to handle it."

Why This Works

Because Jack took a proactive, positive approach, Hailey was receptive to his idea. She could see that Jack was sincere in his offer to teach her and, before concluding their discussion, Hailey asked if Jack would mind if she sat with him every day so that she could learn the job. Jack soon earned Hailey's trust, and because he was willing to help he demonstrated that he was a leader. Two months later, Hailey's father decided to move her to another managerial position and offered Jack a promotion to head the sales team. The moral of this story is that when you stay positive in any situation, good things can happen.

Something to Think About

If other teams are receiving additional training from their bosses to help them do their jobs better, if their bosses hold regular meetings to keep them informed, or if their bosses do other things you wish your incompetent boss would do, speak up. Mention to your boss that you heard another team received some additional training and state that you'd like to receive the same training. If you'd like your boss to hold more meetings, ask for them. Tell your boss what you'd like in specific terms. You'll not only increase the probability that you'll receive what you ask for, you'll help your boss develop valuable skills. Remember to always document your conversations. In the event that your requests fall on deaf ears and you decide to take the next step by going above your boss's head, the documentation will strengthen your case.

Applying the Approach

Apply the following principles when dealing with an incompetent boss:

- Whether it's a new hire or a seasoned veteran who's just plain incapable of performing well, try to adapt to the situation by doing the best job you can.

- Learn to look at the bright side of working for someone who's incompetent: you'll become more independent and self-reliant. You're developing an important skill set when you begin making decisions rather than relying on your boss.

- No matter how you feel about your incompetent boss, never complain about the situation.

- Look for teaching opportunities that will help your boss.

- Show that you want to help. You'll gain your boss's trust and are likely to be treated more as a confidant than an employee.

- If your boss makes a poor decision that affects you, speak up, explain how the decision affects you, and politely suggest that you'd like to be included in making these types of decisions.

- There's no guarantee that your boss will be open to that idea, but you'll get your point across about how the decision affected you.

- Always focus on doing your best job no matter the circumstances under which you work.

How to Deal with an Inconsistent Boss

Terri was never certain how her boss, Greg, was going to act toward her and, once again, he proved how inconsistent he was. Yesterday he praised Terri for doing a great job on a report she was working on. Then, this morning, he stopped by her desk, looked at the report, and told her he was displeased with the way she was putting it together. She opened her mouth in amazement, thinking that nothing had changed with regard to her work from yesterday to today, so how come the great work she did yesterday was not so great today? She shook her head as Greg walked away.

Working for an inconsistent boss can wear on you. Inconsistent bosses are unpredictable. You never know where you stand. One day he's singing your praises, the next he's berating you. They don't think before they speak, because if they did they'd recognize how erratic their behavior is. She may be in a good mood today, but look out tomorrow when her mood heads south. This type of boss may be your best supporter or your biggest detractor, depending on the time of day, the day of the week … or whatever bolsters or bothers this boss. The problem is that you never know how they're going to treat you so you walk on eggshells all day every day. And inconsistent bosses really don't realize they're this way.

The best advice for working for an inconsistent boss is to develop a thick skin and don't take anything they say personally. This type of boss treats everyone this way. It's not about you. It's about what mood they're in at the moment they cross your path. If you know your boss is having a bad day, limit your communication, or ... if you can, steer clear altogether. But this isn't to say that you should always accept the bad behavior. If your boss praises your work and then criticizes you for the same work, why not speak up? You now have a concrete example to share with your boss. Explain how hearing two versions makes you confused. You may or may not gain a better understanding as to why your boss treats you this way, but you should be able to clearly define the problem and offer a compromise that will lead to a resolution. But understand that the resolution may only be temporary or apply to this particular type of situation. Inconsistent bosses may not be inclined to change their ways because they're probably hard wired this way.

Terri decided to speak to Greg and let him know how perplexing his behavior was. It was one thing that his moods changed with the wind. It was another thing that he praised her work one day and criticized it the next.

Step 1: Think First

Terri thought about telling Greg that he was inconsistent, but she realized this was the way he was and that, in all likelihood, he wasn't capable of changing. So she decided to speak to him specifically regarding his comments about the report, hoping that by doing so he might have an aha moment about how he came across.

Step 2: Gain a Better Understanding

When Greg walked over to her later that afternoon, Terri said: "Greg, I wanted to ask you about your opinion on the report I've been working on for you. Yesterday you complimented me on my work, yet this morning you told me you weren't happy with the way I'm compiling it. *Nothing has changed with my work from yesterday to today. What you said confused me.*

Now I'm not sure how you feel about it." (**"I" phrase**) Terri looked directly at Greg when she spoke, making sure she sounded assertive.

"I guess I was in a bad mood this morning," he replied.

"Oh, I can see how that would affect the way you spoke to me," Terri offered. (**understanding**) She continued to make eye contact, glancing away occasionally.

"Let me look at the report now," Greg said.

"Sure." Terri handed him the paperwork.

Greg looked at the report and then said, "It looks fine."

"Do you understand, though, how confusing it was to me when yesterday my work was good and this morning it wasn't?" Terri asked to clarify.

"Yeah, I do," he answered.

Step 3: Define the Problem

Terri defined the problem for Greg. "Hearing two different versions about the quality of the report created a problem for me since I didn't know where I stood with you and I didn't know how to proceed."

Step 4: Offer Your Best Solution

Terri continued: "Greg, you mentioned you were in a bad mood this morning and that's why you said you weren't happy with my work. *Going forward, could I ask you not to comment on my work if you're in a bad mood?*" (**compromise**) Terri then smiled and chuckled to let Greg know that she wasn't taking his negative comment too seriously.

"I'll try to remember that," Greg said, smiling back at her. "I do understand how confusing I must have sounded."

Step 5: Agree on the Resolution

"Thanks for acknowledging that." (**resolution**) Because Terri felt comfortable speaking to Greg, she joked: *"I enjoy working for you, so just stay away if you're going to harp on my work, okay?"*

They both laughed, and Terri was happy she spoke up because even though she knew Greg was incapable of changing his personality, she felt empowered.

Why This Works

Terri spoke up mainly to get what was bothering her off her chest. She was confident that she was doing a good job on the report, and it bothered her that Greg had said one thing yesterday and another today. She had worked for him for a while and had learned to work around his unpredictable behaviors, but when he directly criticized her work she decided to confront him. Because Terri spoke confidently, she was able to make him understand how confusing his comments were. Then she took a more lighthearted approach in asking Greg to refrain from commenting on her work when he was in a bad mood. And, since Terri's comfort level with Greg was solid, she was able to end the conversation by joking with him. Terri wasn't sure if he would take her seriously so if the same situation happened again, she planned to speak up immediately and ask him to tell her specifically what he was displeased with.

Something to Think About

If you work for an inconsistent boss, your best bet is to develop a good relationship in which you'll feel comfortable addressing the inconsistencies. Your conflict resolution conversations will be more productive if you're able to speak candidly, take a light-hearted approach and, as Terri did, joke about the situation with your boss. But even if you don't feel comfortable joking around, getting on this type of boss's good side will definitely improve your outlook and attitude.

Applying the Approach

Apply the following principles when dealing with an inconsistent boss:

- Don't take it personally! This type of boss is inconsistent with everyone, from their employees to their peers to their bosses. It's not about you.

- Just make sure that if your boss compliments you one day and criticizes you the next, that the criticism isn't warranted.

- If criticism isn't warranted, remind your boss that yesterday he complimented you. Then ask him or her to tell you specifically what's wrong with your work.

- If this type of behavior continues to occur, take your conversation a step further and enter into a conflict resolution discussion with your boss. Explain how the inconsistent behavior and comments are confusing to you.

- Ask your boss if he or she understands why it's confusing to you and, then, define the problem you have with the inconsistent behavior.

- Offer a compromise and gain agreement.

- Understand, though, that your resolution will most likely only last a short time. Your boss's inconsistent behavior is apt to recur again.

How to Deal with a Micromanaging Boss

Erica groaned when she saw Dan, her boss, walk over to her desk. She knew he had come to check on her progress on a bid she was completing for a customer. Dan had seemed reticent when he asked her to create the bid and that was because he didn't trust any of his employees to do their work without him hovering over them. Erica's coworker made a humming noise and whispered, "Here comes the helicopter again." Erica smiled, but she wished Dan would have confidence in her abilities.

If you work for a micromanaging boss, then you know how irritating it can be when he or she hovers over you, doesn't trust that you know how to do your job, or feels you need guidance on every assigned task. Micromanagers scrutinize your every move, question your decisions, and give unsolicited help. They don't like to delegate because they don't trust that the work will get done to their expectations. When they do delegate, like Dan, they spend their time looking over your shoulder. New managers may be prone to micromanaging simply because of their lack of confidence. They want to make sure they're doing everything correctly and that can translate into breathing down their employees' backs. Veteran bosses may micromanage a new employee until they're confident the employee is capable of performing well. Some bosses, however, micromanage because they don't trust their employees' abilities.

The danger in working for a micromanager is that you may stop thinking for yourself, making decisions, or improving your skills. When any of those things happen, you may stop caring about your work. Don't allow yourself to fall into any of these traps because they'll hinder your development. You can learn to manage your micromanaging boss, and that begins by building a trusting relationship. Show your boss you know what you're doing. Make your contributions and achievements known to him or her. Demonstrate that you're reliable. Communicate more. Ask for additional responsibility. Volunteer to take on extra tasks. If all else fails, sit down and tell your boss how the micromanaging affects you and your ability to complete your work productively.

Erica came up with an idea that, handled properly, could alleviate Dan's need to micromanage and increase his trust in her.

Step 1: Think First

Her plan was to meet with Dan and tell him that she felt proud about her expertise and ability to do her job. She would then define the problem she had with his hovering, discuss his lack of trust, and end the discussion by asking him to assign her additional responsibilities.

Step 2: Gain a Better Understanding

"Dan, what I wanted to talk to you about is that every time you assign me work, you don't seem to trust that I'll do the job correctly. When you hover over my shoulder asking me questions, it causes me to feel that you don't have confidence in me and that bothers me. It also makes me more determined to show you how capable I am of doing a great job." (**"I" phrase**)

"Gee, Erica, I know that you're capable of doing a great job," Dan responded. "I just like to check up on things."

"I didn't think you were trying to upset me on purpose. (**understanding**) But do you understand how that could make me feel that way?" Erica asked.

Dan shrugged his shoulders. "I guess so."

Erica asked: "Is there anything I've done or that I'm doing that makes you feel you can't trust me to complete my work?"

Dan said: "No, you haven't."

Step 3: Define the Problem

"The main problem I have, as I mentioned, is that I don't feel you trust me," Erica explained. "When I get that feeling I know I'm less productive because I'm focusing on why you don't trust me enough to allow me to work independently. I'd like to discuss how I can gain your trust so that you don't second guess everything I do."

"I do trust you," Dan told her.

Step 4: Offer Your Best Solution

"Thank you. Then what I'd like to ask is when you assign me a bid that you allow me to work without coming over to check on me. I promise that if I

run into a problem I'll let you know. I'll also review my work with you when I'm done," Erica offered. **(compromise)**

Step 5: Agree on the Resolution

Dan agreed. "I can do that."

"Awesome! **(resolution)** I'd also like to ask you if you'll consider assigning me one of the customers that you normally work on," Erica said. "I know how important these clients are and that's why you haven't delegated them to us, but I feel certain that I can handle some of the more difficult bids. And I promise to keep you in the loop while I complete them."

Dan took a deep breath, and replied: "I appreciate your confidence. And I know that of all the employees, you could handle the more involved bids. Yes, I'll agree to assign you one of them."

"Dan, I'm so glad I talked to you about this. I really want you to trust that I'm going to do my best for you," Erica told him." *I really enjoy my job and I look forward to handling some additional responsibilities."* **(reconciliation)**

Why This Works

Erica didn't appreciate Dan's micromanaging ways, especially since she knew how to do her job. She could have sounded off and told him to back off but she decided that taking a proactive approach was going to be more productive and beneficial. She explained how his hovering made her feel and added that it also made her more determined to prove to him that she was capable of doing the work. Erica asked him if she'd done something that caused him not to trust her and, when he said no, she defined the problem. Erica offered a compromise that Dan let her to finish her work without interfering, to which he agreed. She ended the discussion by asking for additional responsibilities, assuring Dan that she was capable of handling more difficult bids and that she'd keep him in the loop.

Something to Think About

If you don't feel comfortable talking to your boss, try to show him or her how capable you are. Don't wait for your boss to hover over your shoulder or ask unnecessary questions. Take a proactive approach by keeping your boss informed about the work you're doing. When you do see him or her coming toward you, speak up and provide an update. This should help gain your boss's trust that you're doing what you're supposed to be doing and may lessen the need to micromanage.

Applying the Approach

Apply the following principles when dealing with a micromanaging boss:

- If your boss micromanages your work, try to determine if there's a valid reason. Have you done something that caused your boss to lose trust in you? Are you a new employee who hasn't yet gained your boss's confidence?

- If you can think of a reason for your boss to feel the need to micromanage, work to gain his or her trust and confidence. It may take some time but the need to micromanage should abate as trust builds.

- If you can't think of a valid reason, try to show your boss that you're doing the best job you can.

- Demonstrate that you're dependable.

- Keep your boss in the loop about the work you're doing.

- Speak up about your achievements.

- If you feel your boss will be receptive, ask to take on additional responsibilities.

- If those measures don't ease the micromanaging, then talk to your boss. Explain how the behavior makes you feel.

- Ask your boss if you've done anything to cause that behavior.

- Define the problem you're having with the micromanaging.

- Offer a compromise and work toward a resolution to which you both can agree.

How to Deal with a Noncommunicative Boss

Steve and his team found out from another employee that their company was merging with another company in three months. Though their jobs wouldn't be affected, they were miffed at Helen, their boss, for not letting them know. This wasn't surprising to them, because Helen didn't communicate much with any of them. Still, this news sent them over the top, especially since all the other teams had been informed by their managers during meetings and Steve and his coworkers had to hear about it through the grapevine.

A lack of communication may be caused by various reasons. Perhaps your boss has no people skills. Perhaps, she's shy or aloof and doesn't have the ability to interact well with others. Or, he might be controlling or egotistical and doesn't feel the need to connect with employees. Whatever the reason, noncommunicative bosses don't keep their employees in the loop to share important company news, provide progress reports, or just to find out how their day is going. Noncommunicative managers don't provide feedback, don't explain decisions, and don't act on suggestions. They provide little direction and when they do delegate work they don't take the time to fully explain what they need. Your noncommunicative boss may possess the technical skills to do the job, but doesn't possess the ability to connect with people, so he or she relies on a hands-off style of managing, which can leave you frustrated and unhappy.

Working for a noncommunicative boss may be extremely challenging. Hearing details of what's happening in your company from other people makes you feel that your boss doesn't care enough to keep you informed. When your boss doesn't provide feedback, frustration builds because you feel that your contributions don't matter. This perception can destroy the creativity and enthusiasm of your entire team. However, there is a solution. You can take positive measures to change the situation. This means that you're going to teach your boss how to be a better communicator. Begin by asking questions, lots of them. Engage your boss in conversations. Ask what's going on in the company. Ask your boss how her day is going. Rather than acting on assumptions about your contributions, speak up and ask your boss how you're doing. When you're confused about an assignment, state very clearly what you need to know. Taking positive measures such as these may help your boss improve his interaction with you. But if you're in a situation like Steve, in which your frustration level has gotten the best of you, it's time to sit down with your boss and discuss the situation.

Steve and his coworkers were so upset that they decided to meet with Helen and tell her directly how they felt hearing such important news through the grapevine. But when they were discussing what they were going to say to her, the conversation heated up, so Steve volunteered to speak for the group. They agreed that this would be the best way to handle the discussion.

Step 1: Think First

Steve took a huge step when he volunteered to be the spokesperson for the group. He knew he'd have to remain calm and objective during the discussion. Because he was also upset, he knew this would be difficult. He planned to focus on how Helen's lack of communication affected the group. Steve gave careful thought to the dialogue. When he was confident that he'd be able to speak assertively and stay composed, he told Helen that the team would like to schedule a meeting to discuss the news about the merger. Steve spoke in an upbeat manner, kept his facial expressions neutral, and projected a confident demeanor, which he also maintained throughout the meeting.

Step 2: Gain a Better Understanding

When they gathered in a conference room, Helen said, "Steve mentioned that you wanted to know why I hadn't told you about the company merger. The reason I didn't say anything is that I know very little about it."

Steve spoke up. *"Hearing such important news through the grapevine really bothered us. We felt that we should have heard it from you."* **("I" phrase).**

"As I said, there wasn't much to tell, so I figured I'd wait until I had more news," Helen reiterated.

But Steve wasn't buying it. He knew Helen well enough to feel certain that even when more news was forthcoming she wouldn't bother sharing it with the team. He said, "*We understand your point of view,* **(understanding)** but can you understand why we're upset that we had to hear such important news from other sources?"

"Well, I'm sorry. I guess I didn't realize that it would upset you," Helen offered. "Here's what I know...." She briefly explained what she knew about the merger.

The team members nodded and listened respectfully as Helen repeated the news they had already heard through the grapevine. They cleared up some questions about the information they had heard.

Step 3: Define the Problem

"Thanks, Helen. The problem we have is that we feel you should have been the one to tell us the news rather than our coworkers," Steve told her. Hearing anything through the grapevine is dangerous. As you could tell by our questions, some of the information we heard wasn't even accurate."

"I understand," Helen responded.

Step 4: Offer Your Best Solution

Steve added: "*What we'd like is to have you keep us in the loop about the merger.*" (**compromise**)

Step 5: Agree on the Resolution

Helen said: "I'll be sure to do that."

Steve ended the discussion by saying: "*We appreciate that you'll keep us informed of any news.* (**resolution**) *What happens in our company matters a great deal to each of us, so thank you for understanding.*" (**reconciliation**)

Why This Works

Rather than addressing Helen's general lack of communication, Steve decided the best way to bring up the problem would be to focus on this one instance. He remained upbeat and calm throughout the discussion, while the rest of the team allowed him to handle the dialogue. He asked if she understood why they were upset and, when Helen apologized and told the team what she knew, Steve followed up by defining the problem. Then he stated the compromise very clearly. When Helen agreed, he offered phrases of resolution and reconciliation. Following the meeting, Steve and his coworkers agreed to try to encourage Helen to communicate better. Going forward, they planned to engage her more by asking questions and discussing what was happening in the company as well as in their team.

Something to Think About

Don't wait for the straw to break the camel's back, like Steve and his team did. Take a proactive approach with a noncommunicative boss by initiating conversations. Get to know your boss. Ask questions. Ask for feedback. Speak up when something bothers you. When you become more involved and aware of good communication techniques, you'll become a better communicator. And becoming a better communicator is a lifelong learning process from which everyone can benefit.

Applying the Approach

Apply the following principles when dealing with a noncommunicative boss:

- Rather than stewing or complaining, take a proactive approach. Try to open up the communication block by talking more.
- If your boss doesn't keep you informed about company matters, ask what's going on.
- If your boss doesn't provide feedback, ask for it.
- If your boss doesn't hold regular meetings, ask for them.
- If your boss assigns work to you, ask questions to make sure you fully understand the expectations.
- Take it one step at a time and hopefully you'll be able to teach your boss how to communicate better. If nothing else, you'll make your needs known, as well as improve your own communication skills.
- If all else fails, you'll need to meet with your boss and explain the problems caused by the lack of communication.

- Share specific examples, but don't bombard your boss with too many. You'll get your point across if you stick to one or two.

- Offer a compromise and take joint responsibility for improving communication.

- If, going forward, your boss falls back into old habits, gently remind him or her about your agreement.

How to Deal with a Passive Boss

Corey listened to Kelly, his coworker, as she spoke rudely to a customer. This was Kelly's typical manner of speaking to customers. Although it bugged Corey to have to constantly put up with her poor attitude, he was most upset by the fact that their boss, Kate, allowed the bad behavior to continue. Kate was more interested in being everyone's friend than their boss. Corey liked Kate but wished she would act more like a manager.

Like Kate, passive bosses want to be everyone's friend. They're likeable people, but being likeable doesn't necessarily translate into being a good boss. Actually, this is one of the worst management styles you'll encounter. These bosses allow others to make all decisions, avoid conflict at all costs, don't set high expectations, make excuses for failures, and provide ineffective feedback. As a result, disagreements and problems fester and grow. They don't feel comfortable providing corrective or negative feedback, so they'll speak in generalities. They don't provide training, but assume their employees will bring each other up to speed. They come across as aimless, disengaged people who are afraid to take risks. Basically, these are hands-off managers and, when they do manage, they often resort to passive–aggressive measures, such as giving someone a dirty look rather than talking about what's bothering them and constructively resolving the issue. They hope that their tacit measures will communicate what they're unable to say. Passive bosses are ineffective bosses who, though amiable, will exasperate their employees, particularly those who set high expectations for themselves.

The bottom line is that passive managers don't want to come across as controlling or micromanaging, so they manage through hope. They hope everything will go right, that results will be satisfactory, and that employees will do their jobs well. But, eventually, even employees who do their jobs well are going to grow weary of managing for the manager. If you work for a passive boss, try not to allow your frustration to get the best of you or cause you to stop caring about your work. In spite of your boss's fear of managing, do your job to the best of your ability. Try to help your boss improve his or her skills by speaking up and asking for what you need. If you need additional training, ask for it. If you'd like more specific feedback, tell your boss how you'd like to receive feedback. If you want more hands-on management, state that. And, when another employee continually does something wrong, talk to your boss and explain the consequences of allowing this behavior to continue.

Later that afternoon, Corey took a call from an irate customer who had hung up on Kelly when she became condescending and offensive. Corey did his best to calm the customer down, but after he hung up he decided it was time to have a conversation with Kate. He'd spoken to Kelly in the past, but she hadn't changed her behavior, so he felt he had no choice but to have Kate deal with it. Kate didn't want to cause waves, but this was one time when she was going to have to step up and deal with the problem.

Step 1: Think First

Corey took time to calm down before he confronted Kate. He thought about how to get his point across and decided to focus on how irate the customer was after speaking to Kelly. He planned to state clearly that this behavior could no longer be tolerated. By allowing by Kelly to continue being rude, customers would probably take their business elsewhere.

Step 2: Gain a Better Understanding

Corey took the bull by the horns when he walked into Kate's office. "Kate, something's been bothering me that I haven't said anything about, but I can't sit idly by any longer."

"What's that, Corey?" Kate asked.

Corey sat down, looked directly at Kate and stated assertively: "I know you must hear how Kelly speaks to her customers, yet you never correct her. I'm wondering why you allow her to continue being rude to them?"

Kate shifted uncomfortably. "I just talked to her the other day. I didn't realize she's still being rude."

"I didn't realize you'd spoken to her. I've spoken to her, too, but nothing changed." (**understanding**) Corey continued: *"Can you understand how upsetting it is to have to listen to her abuse her customers day after day?"* (**"I" phrase**)

"Oh, sure I can," Kate responded. "I tried to be very nice when I spoke to her, and I hoped she'd change but evidently she hasn't."

Step 3: Define the Problem

Corey said: "Up until today, I didn't feel that I had the right to say anything to you about it, but this afternoon I had to handle a customer who was so upset she hung up on Kelly rather than continue to be treated rudely. That's where I have a problem. I don't feel I should have to handle her customers after they've become irate."

"I agree. I'll talk to her again," Kate told him.

Step 4: Offer Your Best Solution

Since Corey wasn't confident that Kate would effectively deal with Kelly, he offered a compromise: *"Since this situation involved me, I'll be happy to be present when you speak to her. That way I can relate what happened with the customer and tell Kelly how much it bothered me. Then you can take it from there and tell her how you expect her to treat customers."* (**compromise**)

"Okay, that sounds good," Kate said. "Let me call her in now."

Step 5: Agree on the Resolution

"That would be great," Corey replied. (**resolution**) *"I'm sure that together you and I can handle this to a positive conclusion."* (**reconciliation**)

Why This Works

Corey was very direct in the manner in which he spoke to Kate, which let her know that he wasn't willing to put up with Kelly's bad behavior any longer. He made sure she understood how he felt and then defined the problem he had when he handled Kelly's customer. Because he had no confidence in Kate's ability to deal with the problem, he volunteered to take part in resolving the problem and she readily agreed.

Something to Think About

Don't beat around the bush or tread lightly with a passive boss. This type doesn't want to deal with adversity of any sort, so if you need your boss to deal with something, as Corey did, state clearly and assertively what you need. Offer an example of how you'd like the situation to be handled, which may give your boss some insight and direction. Or, like Corey, volunteer to take part in solving the problem.

Applying the Approach

Apply the following principles when dealing with a passive boss:

- You may not feel it's your job to be your boss's boss but you can help change that. Encourage him or her to become more proactive.

- Rather than sitting by and allowing problems to continue, state very specifically what you need.

- If another employee does something that affects your work, talk to your boss. Speak assertively, say what happened, and explain how it affected you.

- If your boss is likely to say something to pacify you rather than face the problem, don't accept the boss's response unless you're confident he or she will follow through.

- It may be in your best interest to offer to help, as Corey did.

- Stay involved, and continue to speak up about what you need.

How to Deal with a Reactive Boss

Valerie was busy completing a customer order when Denise, her boss, walked over to the team and said, "Hey everyone, I need you to stop what you're doing. I just got word that our VP is going to drop by our office this afternoon. I want each of you to start working on your quarterly reports. When Ms. Barrett comes in, I want her to see that we're on top of things." Denise thought that was a ridiculous request since the quarter wasn't over and the report wasn't even due in the VP's office until a week after the quarter closed. She was about to say something but knowing how reactive Denise was, she put her order aside and began to compile her report. Still, she wondered why that was necessary. Wasn't it more important that she work on customer orders that were due now rather than to begin a report that she couldn't complete?

Some bosses just don't think things through. Rather than being proactive, they react to outside stimuli without employing critical thinking skills. Rather than having contingency plans in place, they jump on issues before analyzing the consequences. When an emergency situation occurs, they immediately move into crisis mode. These types are usually highly emotional, easily frustrated, and may become volatile when incited. They're like sticks of dynamite, easily set off. When something upsets them, they may resort to inappropriate behaviors, such as yelling, slamming things down, or even acting like a toddler having a temper tantrum.

Working for a boss who is reactive can be tiresome, especially if you're a calm and controlled person. These bosses promote a disruptive environment within their work groups. To them, everything is a catastrophe or a potential disaster waiting to happen. When your boss reacts to every outside stimulus before thinking through the situation, he or she wants to take you along for the ride. Try not to hop on or you'll get caught up in the chaos. Employees may grow weary trying to calm a reactive boss and will go overboard trying to fix a problem just to pacify him or her. Learning what triggers the overreaction will enable you to help your boss. Talk to him about creating a contingency plan to offset those types of circumstances. Most likely, your entire team is affected by your reactive boss, so if she continuously makes your work life miserable, it may be in your best interest to speak up as a group. Give specific examples of reactive responses and the effect they had on your team. Provide a clear definition of the problem and offer practical solutions.

Valerie and her coworkers grumbled as they began working on the quarterly reports. "This doesn't even make sense. We don't have the end of month results, so how is this going to impress Ms. Barrett?" "Don't you think it would impress her more if she saw us doing our jobs?" "Once again Denise jumped without thinking." They agreed that Denise's kneejerk reactions were wearing on them. Just last week she overreacted when two employees called in sick, making the rest of the team take on all of their work rather than analyzing what actually needed to be done. Valerie said, "I think it's time we talked to her. Making us jump through unnecessary hoops is ridiculous. I'll do the talking as long as all of you back me up." The group agreed, and together they walked into Denise's office.

Step 1: Think First

Valerie did some quick thinking as they walked. She wanted to present herself as calm, controlled, and respectful when she made the point that working on the quarterly reports when they had customers' orders to complete didn't make any sense. She also quickly came up with a compromise she hoped Denise would accept.

Step 2: Gain a Better Understanding

"Denise, we wanted to talk to you about the quarterly reports you asked us to start working on for Ms. Barrett," Valerie spoke confidently, matching her facial expressions and demeanor to the manner in which she spoke.

"Sure, what's up?" Denise looked surprised to see all five of her employees in her office.

"We'd like to know if this was something Ms. Barrett requested us to do," Valerie queried.

Denise answered: "Well, no. It was my idea. I want her to see what a well-oiled machine we are."

Valerie spoke thoughtfully. "Do you think that's necessary when we all have customer orders to complete? If we put those aside to start our reports we may have some unhappy customers. Shouldn't they take precedence over a report that we can't even complete at this time?"

"I didn't realize you all had completion dates looming," Denise said.

Step 3: Define the Problem

"We do, and it's causing a problem. *When you asked us to drop what we're working on to start the reports that aren't due yet we felt frustrated,*" Valerie said. **("I" phrase)** *"I mean, we do understand that you want our team to look good, but if that means upsetting customers how good will we look to them?"* **(understanding)**

"Not very," Denise pondered.

Step 4: Offer Your Best Solution

Valerie continued: *"Sometimes we feel that you react to whatever is happening at the moment and that causes a lot of frustration for us.* **("I" phrase")** *Do you think that before you ask us to drop whatever we're doing you could first discuss the situation with us? Then we can all put our heads together and give you additional input that will help you decide the best course of action. Had you known we had customer orders we wouldn't be here talking to you."* **(compromise)**

"I'm sorry, guys. I know that sometimes I fly off the handle. I'll try not to do that in the future. I think your suggestion that we talk about issues is valid." Denise seemed genuinely sorry.

Step 5: Agree on the Resolution

"We appreciate that. **(resolution)** *We all want to do our best for you but also for our customers."* **(reconciliation)** Valerie felt proud of the manner in which she handled the conversation.

"I know you do," Denise responded.

"And about starting the quarterly reports, do you still want us to start those or should we complete our customer orders?" Valerie asked.

"No, get your orders done first," Denise told her. "Then if you're able, start working on the reports."

Why This Works

Even though Denise looked a little blindsided when the entire work group showed up in her office, having Valerie be the spokesperson helped keep the conversation positive and productive. Valerie was careful in the way in which she spoke, first asking questions to help Denise understand that her request was not practical. Then, she defined the problem, both in this instance and in general. She offered a compromise that was constructive. Denise took responsibility for overreacting and agreed to the compromise. Going forward, the group agreed that next time she jumped without thinking, they'd respectfully remind her of their agreement to discuss the matter.

Something to Think About

Just because your boss is reactive doesn't mean you have to emulate that characteristic. It may be easier for you to comply than to take the time to discuss alternatives, but if you fall into the habit of continually jumping at your boss's every whim, you'll likely become frustrated. When that happens, you're going to stop enjoying your work and your attitude is going to change. So be proactive. Talk to your boss about how the constant overreactions are making it difficult for you to complete your job in an efficient and effective manner.

Applying the Approach

Apply the following principles when dealing with a reactive boss:

- Don't allow yourself to be pulled onto the wild ride that they can take you on.
- If it only happens occasionally and you're able to comply without jeopardizing your work, just take a deep breath and don't allow your anxiety to get the best of you.
- Don't get in the habit of constantly mollifying a boss who consistently displays a kneejerk response.
- If you can figure out what triggers your boss's overreaction, come up with a contingency plan for that scenario and present it to him or

her. Show that you want to be part of the solution, and your boss is apt to listen to you.

- When you tell your boss how the reactiveness affects you, it shouldn't be too difficult to get him or her to understand your point of view.

- Reactive bosses probably realize they're this way and are likely to be open to your compromise about working together to come up with the best solutions.

How to Deal with an Unethical Boss

Brittany worked in the billing department handling past due accounts. She had just hung up from a customer call when Zach, her boss, walked to her cubicle in a panic. "Hey Brit, I need your help for the audit tomorrow. I just found out that Chris is way behind in calling his past due customers. Here's a list of his accounts. I need you to make notes on all these that we've tried calling the customers. Just make up different dates so it doesn't look obvious." Brittany felt uncomfortable doing what amounted to cheating for the audit. She took the list from Zach without saying anything, even though she felt that what he asked her to do was unethical.

It can be extremely uncomfortable when your boss asks you to do something that goes against your judgment. You know right from wrong and wonder why your boss doesn't appear to have the same morals and high standards. Unethical bosses disregard company policy. They feel that rules apply to everyone else and find nothing wrong with bending the rules to suit their needs. They may lie and cheat their way to success. They're masters at distorting the truth. And, their unethical behavior may extend into unlawful conduct through padding expense vouchers, taking home supplies, or taking unauthorized time off, all of which amount to stealing from the company.

So what do you do when you work for an unethical boss? You like your job. You may even like your boss. You just don't like his lack of ethics. Working for an unethical boss can be particularly tough, especially if you're forced to comply or sit idly by knowing that what your boss is doing is wrong. You quickly lose trust in the person for whom you work. When that happens, it's difficult for you to feel good about your job. If your boss is doing something unethical and it doesn't affect you, you'll have to decide whether to ignore it or go to a higher authority. This is always a tough call because going above your boss's head may have negative consequences for you. It may be best to ask someone you trust for advice.

But if the unethical behavior does affect you and your boss asks you to do something you know is wrong, say no. Explain why you're not able to comply. If your boss doesn't ask, but demands that you do something you know is wrong and you're forced to comply, voice your opposition to your boss. Speak calmly and address your concerns. Give your boss a chance to do the right thing. If she still demands you to complete the task, state your opposition in writing. Email your boss and explain why you're uncomfortable performing the task that your boss is requiring you to do. Putting it in writing may serve two purposes: you're protecting yourself and you may make your boss think twice before involving you. When you work for an unethical boss, you have to think of yourself first to avoid negative outcomes. Document every conversation and print any emails or other written material that will back up your claim should you decide to go to a higher authority if the unethical behavior continues.

After thinking about what Zach asked her to do, Brittany decided to tell him that she wasn't comfortable noting accounts just to get a better rating on the audit when she knew the customers hadn't been called. She knew that Zach had no problem with bending the rules to make himself look good and that was one thing. Involving her was another thing altogether, and she didn't want to jeopardize her career for Zach.

Step 1: Think First

Brittany knew she'd have to confront Zach directly and express her concerns. She hoped that by explaining herself he'd understand and make the right decision not to make the notes on the accounts. Brittany knew that she'd have to present herself as strong and unwavering. Otherwise, she wouldn't get her point across.

Step 2: Gain a Better Understanding

She spoke to him in his office, where they could discuss the matter privately. *"Zach, I don't feel comfortable that you asked me to note Chris's accounts.* (**"I" phrase**) *I can understand why you thought about doing that so we look good on the audit.* (**understanding**) I just don't feel I should be asked to make the notes when the customers haven't been called."

"It's no big deal. I asked you because you're the best employee I have, and I know you'll get it done for me." Zach didn't seem fazed about her discomfort.

Brittany said: "Thanks for the compliment. But do you understand why I'm not comfortable doing that?"

"Not really," Zach said.

"Let's say that I make the notes on the accounts when I know Chris hasn't made the calls. Then let's say that the auditor finds out that I was the one who did that." Brittany looked directly at Zach when she said that, holding her head high and keeping a serious and concerned facial expression.

"No one's going to find out," Zach countered.

Step 3: Define the Problem

Brittany laid it out for him. "Here's the problem I have. Let's say that someone does find out. It may be a remote possibility, but it's still a possibility. *Zach, I could get fired for doing that, and I'm not willing to take that chance."* (**"I" phrase**)

"No you won't get fired," Zach told her. "If anything happens I'll stick up for you."

Step 4: Offer Your Best Solution

Brittany didn't back down. She presented a strong compromise. *"Zach, I do not want to do this. If you're asking me, then I'm going to point blank say no. My suggestion is to have Chris make the calls to these customers and note the accounts accordingly."* (**compromise**)

"There's no way he'll be able to get to all of them," Zach answered.

"How about this?" Brittany asked. *"I'll make time this afternoon to help him call his customers."* (**compromise**)

"All right. I'll have Chris start calling right now, and I'll give you the uncompleted list this afternoon," Zach said. "But we need to get them all called."

Step 5: Agree on the Resolution

"We will," Brittany assured him. (**resolution**) *"Zach, you know I'd do almost anything for you, but not something I consider to be wrong. I'm glad you understand."* (**reconciliation**)

Why This Works

Brittany could have noted the account records when Zach asked, but doing so would have made her his partner in crime. Because she stood up for herself, Brittany was able to get him to agree to her compromise. Brittany knew she was taking a risk when commenting about his asking her to note the accounts because he could have responded by ordering her to comply. In that event, she was prepared to send him an email documenting their conversation and reiterating that she felt it was wrong. She was pleased that he backed down and also pleased that their conversation ended on a positive note.

Something to Think About

If you work for a company that doesn't value ethical behavior, it may be in your best interest to move on. When your morals are completely different from those of the company for which you work, you'll be miserable. So, do yourself a favor and start looking for other employment with a company whose ideals align with yours.

Applying the Approach

Apply the following principles when dealing with an unethical boss:

- If you're aware of your boss's lack of ethics but what he or she is doing doesn't affect you, think before deciding how to proceed.

- If you decide to ignore it, stay away from your boss as much as possible. You don't want to give others the impression that you associate with or support this person. Just do your job to the best of your ability.

- If you decide to take it to a higher authority, make sure you have good documentation.

- If your boss directly involves you by asking you to do something you know is unethical, say no.

- Explain why you're not able to perform the task.

- If your boss doesn't give you a choice, confront him or her and state clearly why you don't feel comfortable.

- If your boss doesn't back down, send an email documenting your conversation. In essence, you want to state specifically what your boss has ordered you to do and why you disagree.

- This may cover you in the event that someone else finds out. Of course, you may have some explaining to do as to why you didn't report the incident but you should be able to defend yourself against that claim. After all, if you're ordered to complete a task, you really don't have much choice but to comply.

- Always document every conversation, print any written emails or other material that will back up your claim, and keep your file in a safe place.

6

Powerful Phrases for Situations You Cause

When someone causes a problem for you, choosing powerful phrases and sending appropriate nonverbal messages will help you communicate in a constructive manner, no matter the depth of the problem or the person involved. It will take time to build your confidence, but don't underestimate your ability to handle conflict. If you work through the five steps to effective conflict resolution presented in Chapter 3, even if awkwardly at first, you'll reinforce your skills. When you see successful outcomes, you'll gain confidence in your ability to resolve any problem.

But what happens when you're the cause of a problem? What happens when you offend someone or stick your foot in your mouth and say something inappropriate? If you're aware that you caused a problem, don't ignore it. Take the initiative and head the other person off at the pass before he or she confronts you. Think about what you said and how it may have affected the other person. Decide what you want to say to make amends.

When you speak to the person, the first words out of your mouth should always be a phrase of apology, followed by a definition of the problem: *"I'm so sorry I said derogatory things about your proposal during our meeting."* (**apology**) If you feel it's warranted, offer an explanation: *"Honestly, I didn't realize how it sounded until the words flew out of my mouth. Then, I was too mortified to say anything else."* (**"I" phrase**) It's likely that the other person has the same interpretation as you, so rather than ask questions to gain a better understanding, reiterate your definition of the problem, showing empathy: *"The problem is that I didn't think before I blurted that out, and I understand if you're upset or angry with me."* (**understanding**) Now give the other person a chance to respond. He might say: "Oh, it didn't bother me at all." Or she might reply: "You're darn right. I was angry." Either way, offer a compromise: *"Going forward, I promise that I'll do my best to think before I open my mouth."* (**compromise**) End the conversation with phrases of resolution and reconciliation: *"Thanks for being so nice about this.* (**resolution**) *I want to keep our working relationship strong."* (**reconciliation**) That's all there is to it. When you take the bull by the horns and own up to making a mistake, the response is likely to be positive, the conversation is likely to be quick, and you'll keep all your working relationships strong.

There will be times, though, when something you've said or done bothers another person … and you aren't even aware of it. If the person is skilled in effectively dealing with conflict, your conversation will be resolved by moving through the steps. But what happens when the other person isn't skilled in conflict resolution? In that event, he or she may speak in generalities or resort to passive–aggressive measures, such as ignoring you or giving you an angry look, in which case you're going to have to discern what the problem is. Or, the person might directly confront you in an accusatory tone, yell at you, say something hurtful, or attack your character. The point of these personal attacks is to make you feel bad and put you in your place. And, that's usually the result.

When that happens, you'll have difficulty maintaining your composure. Let's face it: We enjoy being on the receiving end of compliments, but we don't enjoy being on the receiving end of criticisms, especially when they're delivered in a spiteful, mean-spirited manner. You may find negative feedback tough to swallow, but you can benefit from it if you take the time to listen, assess it, decide whether it's valid and, if it is, use the feedback as a catalyst for change.

So how do you respond to someone who angrily or emotionally blames you for something? Take a step back, rein in your emotions, and inhale deeply. Think about the feedback with an open mind. Look at the situation from the other person's perspective. Put aside your pride. Take the words to heart. Whether the feedback is valid, you upset this person and you're going to have to resolve the conflict to move forward. Follow the five steps, and you'll be able to turn the conversation around, resolve the issue, and move on.

Resolving Conflict: The Wrong Way

Jodie worked as a reporter for a local newspaper and was editing an article she had written when Ted, her coworker, walked into her cubicle. Catching her off guard, he angrily lashed out: "You always ignore me when I ask you questions or try to talk to you. I don't understand why you do that to me, and I'm really sick of it. I don't deserve to be treated this way, and it makes you look like you think you're better than me. It's rude."

He glared at Jodie, who was aghast at what he said. She prided herself on getting along with her coworkers and on being helpful and supportive toward all of her colleagues, including Ted. She was so appalled she shot back: "I don't know what you're talking about, and I certainly don't appreciate what you're saying. I don't always ignore you. If I don't answer your questions maybe it's because you ask stupid ones that don't warrant answers. Did you ever think of that? And, by the way, I'm not rude. I get along with everyone. Everyone else, that is."

Ted spoke brusquely: "Oh, you think so! Well I beg to differ with you. And I'm sorry if you think I ask stupid questions. Maybe if you got off your high horse once in a while you'd be nicer to people. And yes. You are rude!" He didn't wait for an answer, but rather stomped off, leaving Jodie stewing about his nerve speaking to her as he did.

Why This Doesn't Work

When Ted confronted Jodie in an antagonistic manner, she immediately became defensive and aggressively defended herself, rather than taking time to recover, regroup, and think how to best respond. That wouldn't have taken long to do, but she spoke without thinking and, by doing so, she spoke to him as he had spoken to her, lashing out angrily. Until now, Jodie had always prided herself on being able to get along with her co-workers. She felt she communicated well with them and was able to resolve any problem effectively. But this was different, she convinced herself. This was a direct attack on her character, and she had the right to defend herself. Jodie concluded that Ted caught her off guard and, as a result, she didn't have time to prepare herself to have a constructive conversation. She tried to convince herself that she had a right to speak to him as he spoke to her, yet she regretted losing control.

Later, after thinking about what he said, Jodie admitted to herself that on occasion she had pretended that she didn't hear him. But that was because he asked her questions without noticing that she was at a crucial point in her writing. When she was so involved with what she was working on, redirecting her attention to answer his question would have caused her to lose her concentration. So, at times, she pretended not to hear. She wanted to explain that to Ted but she was still angry with the manner in which he blasted her—and embarrassed that she lost her composure—so she ignored him the rest of the day. The next day they were cool to each other. As time went on, Jodie kept replaying what Ted said and, every time she did, she'd remind herself that she had a right to feel angry. Consequently, their working relationship was strained.

Step 1: Think First

You know that before responding to any statement or question you should always think first and choose your words wisely, but that isn't always easy to do when someone confronts you with negative feedback. It may be nearly impossible when that person also attacks your character because you become emotional and feel hurt or angry. Your likely response, like Jodie's, is to stick up for yourself. You want to immediately counteract the accusation, but the problem with sticking up for yourself without thinking first is that you're going to react defensively. When you lose control, you're apt to continue down that path, saying things that you'll later regret. And, when you do that, it's going to be nearly impossible to recover and enter into a productive conflict resolution dialogue. Anger and resentment usually accompany defensiveness, and you'll be more likely to focus on those emotions than to think logically. But thinking logically is what you must train your mind to do when someone confronts you, especially in a poor manner.

So, take a moment to recover from the onslaught of words. Pause before you respond. Bite your tongue if necessary. Calm your thoughts and compose yourself. Focus on listening carefully without interrupting. Your gut reaction will be to interrupt, explain, or disagree. Don't. No matter the means in which the message is conveyed to you, listen attentively. Understand that the person giving you feedback may not have learned the components of effectively resolving conflicts, so always allow the person to finish without interrupting.

As you're listening, maintain a neutral or concerned facial expression. Listen actively by maintaining eye contact, but don't overreact by raising your eyebrows, opening your mouth, or clenching your teeth. Breathe deeply to help you maintain your composure. Keep your body language relaxed and refrain from crossing your arms in front of you or tensing up.

No matter how much you might want to, don't respond. And don't allow yourself to become defensive. Take a moment to process what the person is telling you. If, like Ted, the person uses the words "always" or "never," ignore those words because they're usually voiced in anger or frustration. Ask yourself what the person is really telling you. Quickly assess whether the feedback is valid. Whatever you decide, the other person has a problem, so you'll need to resolve the issue. Think how best to respond, then continue the dialogue using the five-step process to reach an agreement.

Key Points

Practice the following to help you think first:

- Focus on listening carefully without interrupting. Allow the person to get it all out.
- When you're listening, don't react. Keep your facial expressions neutral, and don't show anger or shock. Keep your demeanor relaxed, and refrain from crossing your arms or tensing your body.
- Don't become defensive.
- Stay calm and composed, as this will help you process the information logically.
- Pause before responding.
- Always think before you speak. Assess the feedback and plan your response.
- Decide how to respond, focusing on following the five-step process.

Taking Time to Think About a Conflict

Jodie worked as a reporter for a local newspaper and was editing an article she had written when Ted, her coworker, walked into her cubicle. Catching her off guard, he angrily lashed out: "You always ignore me when I ask you questions or try to talk to you. I don't understand why you do that to me, and I'm really sick of it. I don't deserve to be treated this way, and it makes you look like you think you're better than me. It's rude."

He glared at Jodie, who was aghast at what he said. Her immediate thought was to defend herself against his accusation, especially when he said she always ignored him because she knew that wasn't true. Just as she felt her own anger bubbling up, Jodie composed herself. She didn't respond, and she didn't react. Rather, she projected a concerned facial expression and placed her hands in her lap when he was speaking. She calmed her racing thoughts by breathing deeply and slowly as she processed the negative feedback. She knew that Ted was partially correct; on occasion, she had ignored him. However, she only did that when switching gears to answer him would have caused her to lose her train of thought. She thought about how to respond in a constructive manner so that they could resolve the conflict effectively.

Step 2: Gain a Better Understanding

It doesn't matter how the message was delivered or whether you agree. You listened carefully, processed the message, and thought about how you want to proceed with the dialogue. Say something positive to put the other person at ease: *"I appreciate that you let me know about this. Let's talk about it."* (**compromise**) Or *"Thank you for sharing that with me. I'd like to discuss it further."* (**compromise**) Keep in mind that even if you don't agree with the feedback, something you said or did prompted the criticism. Delving further and making sure you understand where the person is coming from will help you know what initiated the feedback and how to proceed.

Not only do you want to gain a better understanding of the problem, it's important to make sure that you both have the same understanding. You'll want to know what the key issue is, so you'll likely have to wade through the emotional words that are tied to the core message. Ask open-ended questions to gather more information: "Can you give me some examples of when this happened?" Ask closed-ended questions to clarify information: "Are you saying that during our meeting yesterday I interrupted you when you were speaking?" It's important that you clear up any confusion or misinterpretation before proceeding to define the problem.

It's also important to remain objective when asking or answering questions. This isn't the time to defend or rationalize what prompted the negative feedback. When you feel that you both have the same understanding, offer a phrase of apology if you feel that will help: *"I'm really sorry that you had to come to me about this."* (**apology**) When you offer an apology in that manner, you aren't necessarily taking responsibility for causing the problem. Rather you're merely sharing your regret for whatever prompted the conversation. Then offer a phrase of understanding: *"I'd be upset, too, if I felt as you do."* (**understanding**)

Pay attention to the nonverbal message you're sending, as well as the one you're receiving. Keep your facial expressions and body language relaxed and neutral. Make eye contact and nod to show that you understand what the other person is saying. Watch for signs that the other person is calming down or is still emotional. By projecting a calm, composed demeanor you'll help the other person calm down as well.

You should now be prepared to define the problem, but if you need more time to process the feedback say so: "I'd like to think about it and get back to you later today." Make sure that you do get back to the person when you say you will; otherwise he or she is likely to become even angrier. But it's certainly okay to delay the conversation if you need time to think about the situation, especially when someone catches you off guard and you're ill prepared to continue the dialogue.

Key Points

Practice the following when gaining a better understanding:

- Tell the person you appreciate the feedback, no matter how it was delivered.
- Ask open-ended questions if you need to gather more information.
- Ask closed-ended questions to clarify the information and clear up misunderstandings.
- Remain objective when asking and answering questions.
- Before you attempt to define the problem, offer a phrase of apology if you feel it's warranted. Saying something like: *"I'm sorry this happened,"* (**apology**) doesn't mean you're taking the blame for the problem. Rather, it shows that you regret the problem.
- If you need time to think about the best way to respond, say so. Tell the person you'd like to think about it and discuss it later.

Gaining a Better Understanding of the Situation

Jodie smiled and showed concern in her facial expression when she said: *"Ted, I appreciate what you're saying, and I'm glad you came to me about this so that we can discuss what's going on."* **compromise)**

Ted seemed to relax a bit.

Jodie had already acknowledged to herself that on occasion she had ignored Ted, so she asked a clarifying question: "Are you saying that I always ignore you when you ask a question?"

Ted admitted: "Well, not always. But a lot of the time, yes, you do ignore me. I know you have to hear me, but you act like you don't."

Jodie nodded thoughtfully. *"I'm really sorry that you had to come to me about this. I'd be upset, too, if I thought someone was ignoring me."* **(apology, understanding)** She was pleased to observe that Ted smiled and visibly calmed down.

Jodie felt prepared to continue the conversation, so she added: "Why don't you sit down? *I'm sure that by talking through this, we'll be able to resolve the issue."* **(compromise)**

Step 3: Define the Problem

When you feel that you and the other person are on the same page and have cleared up any misunderstandings, you can define the problem. This will be handled a little differently when someone has confronted you than when you confront someone else. When someone's come to you about something you said or did, it's important to define the problem from both perspectives: "Here's how you view it … and here's how I view it." By defining both sides of the issue, you put yourself on a level playing field. You can then work through the issue to a satisfactory agreement.

First, reiterate the other person's concerns, as you define the problem from his or her point of view: *"I understand you feel that on occasion I interrupt you during meetings."* **(understanding)** Gain agreement: "Is that correct?" Then state your point of view: "After thinking about it, you're right. I have interrupted you on occasion." Next, provide your supporting reasons: "But here's why…." State your reasons as an "I" phrase to show how you feel: *"We have a time commitment during our meetings, and I get perturbed when you take too much time and I don't get to speak."* **("I" phrase)** If you don't agree with the claim, define the problem from your point of view and offer a phrase of compromise: "I have never intentionally interrupted you, *but let's talk about it.*" **(compromise)**

Speak respectfully as you define the problem, as that will pave the way for an open discussion that will lead to an agreeable resolution. Show concern in your facial expression. Don't become emotional, but rather maintain a neutral tone of voice and keep a relaxed demeanor.

Key Points

Practice the following when defining the problem:

- Recap the other person's concerns: "I understand that you feel that...." This defines and clarifies the problem from the other person's viewpoint.
- Define the problem from your vantage point.
- If, after assessing the feedback as correct, state an agreement: "After thinking about it, I agree with you."
- If you agree, but want to provide additional information, say: "Here's the reason why."
- If, after assessing the feedback as incorrect, state your view: "I appreciate what you're saying, but I have to disagree."
- Offer a phrase of compromise: "*Let's talk about it.*"
- Maintain concern in your facial expression, and speak slowly and calmly.

Defining the Problem to Clarify the Points of View

Jodie stated: "*I understand you feel that at times I've ignored you when you asked me a question, correct?*" **(understanding)**

Ted nodded.

Jodie continued, speaking in a calm voice and maintaining a concerned facial expression: "After thinking about it, I have to agree with you. At times I have ignored you. But here's why. When I'm in the middle of writing an article I have to get my thoughts down as they come to me, otherwise I'll lose them. When you've asked me a question at that moment, I've kept typing rather than take the chance of losing my thought because I can assure you, once it's gone it's gone for good. *And when that happens, I become frustrated.*" She smiled. **("I" phrase)**

Ted said: "Oh, that's happened to me too."

"If that's happened to you, then you can understand my frustration." **(understanding)**

"I can."

Step 4: Offer Your Best Solution

When you define the problem from both vantage points and show respect for the other person's point of view, you create a dialogue in which the other person should be open to hearing your proposed solution. As soon as you agree on the definition of the problem, don't belabor or rehash the point. Be prepared to offer your best solution. Or, if the other person offers a solution first, quickly analyze it and either agree to it or offer a compromise.

Remain flexible during the give-and-take exchange, especially if you strongly disagree on the best solution. Don't allow the discussion to sidetrack or backtrack. Work through any differences by showing that you're willing to cooperate, because cooperation lends itself to collaboration. If the discussion stalls, suggest that you each restate your best solution and together analyze the consequences of each. If worse comes to worse, you may have to agree to disagree and put the issue to rest, particularly if the other person isn't willing or able to cooperate or understand your position on the issue.

Key Points

Practice the following when offering your best solution:

- As soon as you agree on the definition of the problem, offer your best solution.

- In the event that the other person offers a solution first, quickly analyze it.

- If you agree to it, say so. Otherwise, offer a compromise.

- Remain flexible while negotiating the resolution.

- Show that you're willing to cooperate by discussing alternatives to the proposed solution.

- Stay on track with the discussion. If the conversation begins to backtrack, bring it back to solving the problem. You already agreed on the definition so there is no need to rehash that part of the dialogue.

- If you're not able to resolve the issue, you may have to agree to disagree.

Offering Your Best Solution to the Problem

Ted suggested: "I'm sorry. From now on I won't ask you any questions when I see that you're typing."

Jodie quickly thought about his proposed solution and said: *"No, I don't want you to do that. How about this? If you come in and I'm typing, wait for me to get my thought down. And if I'm too involved to help, I'll give you a sign to let you know it isn't a good time. Does that sound okay to you?"* **(compromise)**

Ted said: "That works for me."

Step 5: Agree on the Resolution

When you agree to the proposed solution, offer a phrase of resolution. You might say: *"Great. I'm glad we worked this out."* (**resolution**) There will be times when you're not going to agree, but you can still offer a phrase of resolution: *"I'm sorry we aren't able to agree on this, but I'm still glad we talked it out. Let's respect each other's opinion, and let it go at that."* (**resolution**)

After offering a phrase of resolution, end your discussion by offering a phrase of reconciliation: *"I enjoy working with you and wouldn't want any misunderstandings to come between us."* (**reconciliation**) In the event you're unable to come to an agreement, end the discussion by offering an alternate phrase of reconciliation: *"I'm sorry we can't come together on this. (**resolution**) I value our working relationship and hope that we can move forward and put this issue to rest."* (**reconciliation**)

Key Points

Practice the following when agreeing on the resolution:

- After you agree on the solution, offer a phrase of resolution.
- Follow that with a phrase of reconciliation.
- If you were unable to agree, offer a phrase of resolution suggesting that you agree to disagree and let go of the issue.
- Follow with a phrase of reconciliation stating that you want to move forward without letting this situation come between you.

Gaining Agreement on the Resolution

Jodie followed up by saying: *"Ted, I'm really glad that you came to me about this. I'm sorry that I've ignored you, and I'm glad we found a solu-*

tion that'll work for both of us. (**resolution**) *I think our conversation will make our relationship stronger knowing that we can resolve any differences."* (**reconciliation**)

Resolving Conflict: The Right Way

Jodie worked as a reporter for a local newspaper and was editing an article she had written when Ted, her coworker, walked into her cubicle. Catching her off guard, he angrily lashed out: "You always ignore me when I ask you questions or try to talk to you. I don't understand why you do that to me, and I'm really sick of it. I don't deserve to be treated this way, and it makes you look like you think you're better than me. It's rude."

He glared at Jodie, who was aghast at what he said. Her immediate thought was to defend herself against his accusation, especially when he said she always ignored him because she knew that wasn't true. Just as she felt her own anger bubbling up, Jodie composed herself. She didn't respond, and she didn't react. Rather, she projected a concerned facial expression and placed her hands in her lap when he was speaking. She calmed her racing thoughts by breathing deeply and slowly as she processed the negative feedback. She knew that Ted was partially correct; on occasion, she had ignored him. However, she only did that when switching gears to answer him would have caused her to lose her train of thought. She pondered about how to respond in a constructive manner so that they could resolve the conflict effectively.

Jodie smiled and showed concern in her facial expression when she said: *"Ted, I appreciate what you're saying, and I'm glad you came to me about this so that we can discuss what's going on."* (**compromise**)

Ted seemed to relax a bit.

Jodie had already acknowledged to herself that on occasion she had ignored Ted, so she asked a clarifying question: "Are you saying that I always ignore you when you ask a question?"

Ted admitted: "Well, not always. But a lot of the time, yes, you do ignore me. I know you have to hear me but you act like you don't."

Jodie nodded thoughtfully. *"I'm really sorry that you had to come to me about this. I'd be upset, too, if I thought someone was ignoring me."* **(apology, understanding)** She was pleased to observe that Ted smiled and visibly calmed down.

Jodie felt prepared to continue the conversation so she added: "Why don't you sit down? *I'm sure that by talking through this, we'll be able to resolve the issue."* **(compromise)**

Jodie stated: *"I understand you feel that at times I've ignored you when you asked me a question, correct?"* **(understanding)**

Ted nodded.

Jodie continued, speaking in a calm voice and maintaining a concerned facial expression: "After thinking about it, I have to agree with you. At times I have ignored you. But here's why. When I'm in the middle of writing an article I have to get my thoughts down as they come to me, otherwise I'll lose them. When you've asked me a question at that moment, I've kept typing rather than take the chance of losing my thought because I can assure you, once it's gone it's gone for good. *And when that happens, I become frustrated."* She smiled. **("I" phrase)**

Ted said: "Oh, that's happened to me too."

"If that's happened to you, then you can understand my frustration." **(understanding)**

"I can."

Then Ted suggested: "I'm sorry. From now on I won't ask you any questions when I see that you're typing."

Jodie quickly thought about his proposed solution and said: *"No, I don't want you to do that. How about this? If you come in and I'm typing, wait for me to get my thought down. And if I'm too involved to help, I'll give you a sign to let you know it isn't a good time. Does that sound okay to you?"* (**compromise**)

Ted said: "That works for me."

Jodie followed up by saying: *"Ted, I'm really glad that you came to me about this. I'm sorry that I've ignored you, and I'm glad we found a solution that'll work for both of us.* (**resolution**) *I think our conversation will make our relationship stronger knowing that we can resolve any differences."* (**reconciliation**)

Why This Works

When Ted lashed out at Jodie, her first instinct was to defend herself. She felt herself becoming angry but, because she had learned the skills to effectively resolve conflict, she quickly composed herself, got back on track, and moved through the five-step process. Even though Ted had approached her, Jodie led the discussion. She maintained her composure and showed through her facial expressions and body language that she was concerned, that she respected Ted, and that she wanted to find an agreeable solution. She wasn't afraid to agree with Ted's view that she had on occasion ignored him and, because she explained why she had done so, Ted gained a better understanding. The manner in which Jodie spoke throughout the conversation kept their dialogue positive and constructive, and they were quickly able to reach an agreement. While this was a fairly simple problem between two coworkers, following the five-step process will help you work through any problem, small or large.

Something to Think About

When someone gives you negative feedback, think of it as a positive. If it's accurate, it provides a growth opportunity; if it isn't accurate, it provides an opportunity to strengthen your conflict resolution skills. Remember no one is perfect. We all have blind spots when it comes to our strengths and weaknesses. And, we all do things that bother other people. The best teacher often comes in the form of negative feedback, but only when we take the time to analyze what we're hearing. So the next time you're on the receiving end of negative feedback, give yourself a reality check. Listen. Analyze. Decide whether to accept the feedback. Whatever you decide, the other person still has a problem with you, so work through the five-step process to resolve the conflict. Then ask yourself: Going forward, what can I do differently to avoid this from happening again? When you do that, you'll gain respect as a person who genuinely cares about how you treat others.

ABOUT THE AUTHOR

Renée Evenson is a small business consultant and writer specializing in organizational psychology in the workplace—the roles defining customers, employees, and management and the relationships among them. During her fifteen-year management career at BellSouth Telecommunications, her responsibilities included customer service for the small business market; sales and marketing staff management; staff training and development; training material development; team leadership development; and strategic planning.

After leaving BellSouth, Renée translated her expertise and experience into a writing career. She is the author of *Customer Service 101: Basic Lessons to Be Your Best, Customer Service 201: Managing Your People to Be Their Best, Customer Service Training* (2nd edition), *Award-Winning Customer Service, Customer Service Training 101,* and *Powerful Phrases for Effective Customer Service.*

Renée has written numerous magazine articles on customer, employee, and management relations, and she has been interviewed and featured in several print and radio media. Renée has lived in Chicago, Florida, and New Jersey, but she and her family now enjoy life on Saint Simons Island, Georgia.

Printed in the USA
CPSIA information can be obtained
at www.ICGtesting.com
JSHW031200050524
62550JS00009B/92

9 780814 432983